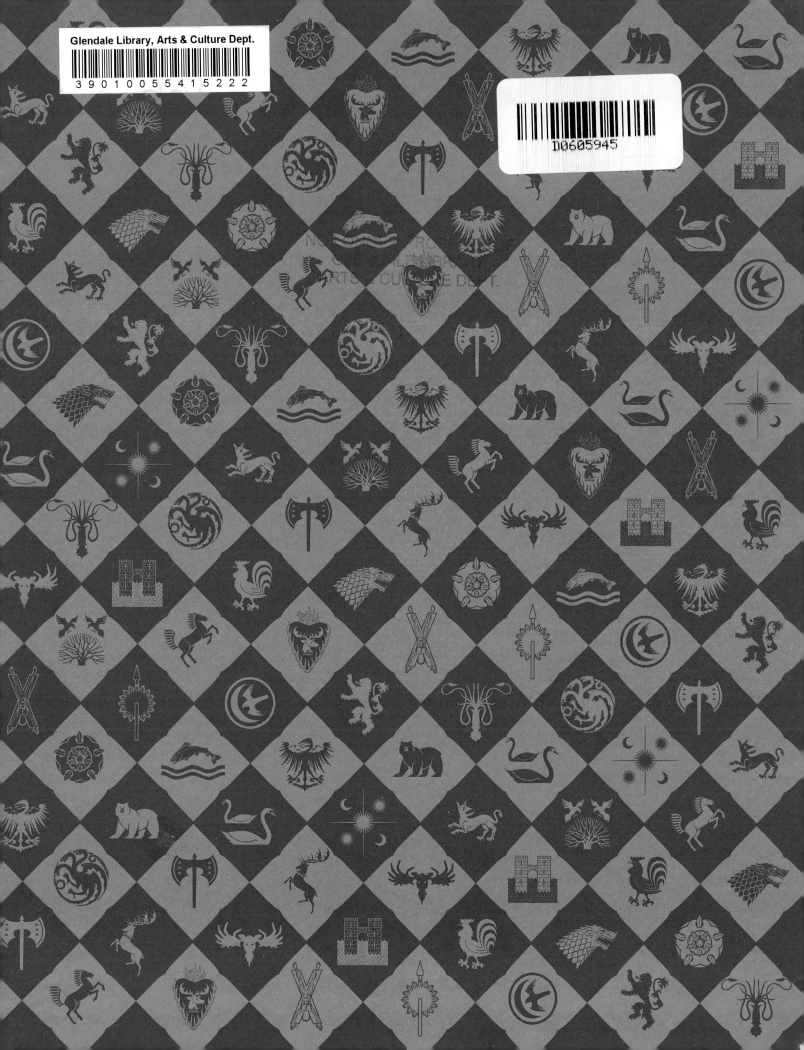

Glendale Library, Arts & Culture Dept.

3 9010 05541522 2

NO LONGER PROPERTY OF
GLENDALE LIBRARY,
ARTS & CULTURE DEPT.

INSIDE HBO'S

GAME OF THRONES™

SEASONS 3 AND 4

C. A. TAYLOR

Foreword by DAVID BENIOFF AND D. B. WEISS

CHRONICLE BOOKS
SAN FRANCISCO

791.4572 TAY

— ACKNOWLEDGMENTS —

It's a strange thing to know in the moment that you are part of something very special. Working on *Game of Thrones* was, without question, one of the best experiences in my career, due in large part to the exceptional cast and crew that I feel genuinely honored to have worked with. For everyone I bothered repeatedly for quotes, stole time from in the height of the insanity and then returned to with more questions, thank you. I would have included every word if the pages could hold them. I have seen the artistry that goes into every element. I remain in awe.

Particular thanks must go to Frank Doelger, Bernie Caulfield, Chris Newman, Michele Clapton, Tom Martin, Deb Riley, and Tommy Dunne who went above and beyond for me. Special thanks also to Joanne Hall, Ide O'Rourke, Adam Chazen, Donna Hughes, and Terry Palmer for helping me with constant queries and pulling the most fantastic visuals.

Alanna Riddell, William Simpson, Annick Wolkan, Naimh Currie, Kate McLaughlin, and Steve Collins: You kept me caffeinated and kept me sane.

Helen Sloan and Bryan Cogman: This book would not exist without you and is better for you. You have my marker and my gratitude.

Cara Grabowski at HBO and Sarah Malarkey at Chronicle, who gave me more patience and guidance then I probably deserved.

Lastly, but never least: George R. R. Martin, for creating this epic story and then giving me far more time than you ever needed to help me explore it, I am truly thankful. David Benioff and Dan Weiss, you gave me an opportunity and invited me in to a world I never expected to see. For everything I have learned, I owe you a debt.

I dedicate this book to my mother, Ruth.

Special thanks to: Joshua Goodstadt, Janis Fein, Cara Grabowski, Stacey Abiraj, Tommy Finkelstein, Vicky Lavergne, Susanna Felleman, Robin Eisgrau, Sarah Malarkey, Michael Morris, Lia Brown, Jeff Campbell, Dean Burrell, Beth Steiner, and Johan Almqvist.

Game of Thrones series photographs by principal unit photographer, Helen Sloan.
Additional photography by unit photographers Macall Polay, Keith Bernstein, Neil Davidson, and Nick Briggs; and by Robert Boake, Niall McEvoy, Colin McCusker, Aoife Warren, and Barrie Gower/BGFX.
Costume illustrations by Michele Clapton.
Game of Thrones main title composition by Ramin Djawadi.
Sheet music visual by Ramin Djawadi and William Marriott.
Concept art by Tobias Mannewitz, Anthony Leonardi III, Nick Ainsworth, and Peter McKinstry.
Sept set model by Aoife Warren.
VFX images by Elastic, Pixomondo, SpinVFX.
Slaver's Bay map by Jacob Taylor.

WWW.HBO.COM
Copyright © 2014 by HOME BOX OFFICE, INC.
All rights reserved. HBO and related trademarks are the property of Home Box Office, Inc.

Library of Congress Cataloging-in-Publication data available.
ISBN 978-1-4521-2218-2
Manufactured in China

Designed by Ryan Corey for Smog Design, Inc.

10 9 8 7 6 5 4 3 2 1

CHRONICLE BOOKS LLC
680 Second Street   ◆   San Francisco, CA 94107   ◆   www.chroniclebooks.com

— CONTENTS —

NO LONGER PROPERTY OF
GLENDALE LIBRARY,
ARTS & CULTURE DEPT.

— FOREWORD —

BY DAVID BENIOFF AND D. B. WEISS

With every great story there is a beginning. For Game of
Thrones, *it began with David Benioff and Dan Weiss reading a
series of epic novels by George R. R. Martin and, with his hard
won blessing, putting together a pitch for the only network they
thought could bring the project to life: HBO.*

*Now, at the end of their fourth successful season, David
and Dan revisit that letter and look back over the milestone
moments for the series.*

C. A. TAYLOR: Reading the pitch letter you sent to HBO in
2006, it's clear you knew you had found something special in
George R. R. Martin's books. You went as far as to bet your
careers on the series' success. (I think you may have won.) Did
you ever imagine that it would be as huge a phenomenon as it has
been?

DAVID BENIOFF AND D. B. WEISS: No. We imagined
a few different kinds of phenomena that it might be. A "thing
that would have been really cool if the only place in the world
that could do it didn't just say no" phenomenon. A "well, we just
wasted three years of our lives and a thousand gallons of hope

on a pilot that tanked and was not picked up" phenomenon. A
"we made a show watched by about a third as many people who
would need to watch it to justify its expense" phenomenon. But
"huge phenomenon" never seemed a likely contender.

CT: Was there a particular moment when you realized what the
show was becoming?

BENIOFF AND WEISS: When (HBO CEO) Richard Plepler
first told us, in confidence, that he needed advanced copies of
a season's episodes for the President of the United States. And

when a friend sent us a video of the line outside the GoT exhibition in New York. And when our mothers stopped asking if we'd found another job yet.

CT: You have often been quoted as saying that one of your main goals for the show was to make it as far as the Red Wedding. What was it about that moment that made it such a key milestone for you?

BENIOFF AND WEISS: Well, the effect it seems to have had on people watching it was the exact same effect it had on us when we first read it. It was perhaps the most powerful feeling a fictional event had ever caused in us. And the thought of bringing that feeling to the screen was very compelling. Basically, we wanted to ruin a lot of people's months.

CT: Looking back over the first four seasons, is there any key episode, scene, or moment that stands out for you as something you are particularly proud of how it turned out?

BENIOFF AND WEISS: It's impossible to pick one, or two. We've been lucky enough to work with a ridiculous number of ridiculously talented people, and their combined efforts have provided the show with an embarrassment of riches.

CT: You both directed episodes for seasons three and four. Was this something you always planned on trying and was it difficult to approach the episode as both writer and director?

BENIOFF AND WEISS: The arguments with the writers were very uncomfortable. Those guys are monumental assholes.

We had always planned on trying it, yeah, if we got to the place where the show was working well and we felt comfortable stepping away for the time it took to do it. And it's been a tremendous amount of fun. By the time we did it, we were lucky enough to be working with people we knew, loved, and trusted. So it was like being tossed into the deep end—but with arm floaties.

CT: Looking to the future, what do you think your biggest challenges will be with the upcoming series?

BENIOFF AND WEISS: Well, every year things get bigger and more ambitious, on the production level. So moving forward, the challenge will always be to see just how much we can shoot and post in time for next year's premiere air date. As far as the story goes . . . the cast list changes on this show. In the first three seasons, it was largely an issue of dealing with expansions, and how to keep an increasingly large number of characters vital and in-play. From the end of season three, the challenge has changed, somewhat—we're in the contraction phase, moving slowly but surely toward an endgame. Now it's more about the ways the show evolves in light of the departures of those characters that are no longer with us. Joffrey's death, for instance—that changes the dynamics of the show's world drastically.

CT: If you could bring back one person from the dead, who would it be?

BENIOFF AND WEISS: We'd have Khal Drogo haul Joffrey, Robb, Cat, and Ned from the underworld on his back. He can probably manage. He's bulked up since he died. If he can't quite do it, Tywin can carry one of them.

[OPPOSITE] *David and Dan observing the filming of a key King's Landing scene.*

__ IN THE WRITER'S ROOM __
INTERVIEW WITH BRYAN COGMAN

Bryan Cogman began working as an assistant for David Benioff and Dan Weiss several years before Game of Thrones *was greenlit. With his encyclopedic knowledge of the show, Bryan acts as the keeper of the* Game of Thrones *bible, offering insight into the backstory and characters when needed. Bryan has written episodes, worked as story editor, and is now co-producer.*

C. A. TAYLOR: You are actively involved in adapting the story from the books to the screen, starting with creating the season outline. How do you approach such a massive task?

BRYAN COGMAN (CO-PRODUCER AND WRITER): For seasons one and two, when we were doing a book a season, I would sit down and summarize each chapter beat by beat and create documents outlining the various character arcs in the book. In later seasons, that changed into me summarizing chapters from various books. After we all digest the book material, David and Dan assign each of the writers a few characters. So I wrote out an outline of Arya's season three—adapting book scenes and coming up with some of my own. Now, 80 percent of this stuff might not ever make the show, but it gives us a starting point. Then, between seasons, we meet in the writer's room for a few weeks, read each other's first outlines, merge them together, throw stuff out, come up with new stuff, and put the main beats up on a board—a rough season emerges from that. From there, we collaborate on a polished and detailed outline on the season, which David and Dan eventually take over and finish up. After this, scripts are assigned and written.

CT: Is there a particular line or scene that you wish you had written?

BC: Yes, it's a scene that I'm credited with writing! Yoren's monologue to Arya in "What Is Dead May Never Die" [season two, Episode 203], in which he relates the story of killing his brother's murderer before joining the Night's Watch and plants the idea in Arya's head of reciting a "vengeance prayer" each night of people she wants to kill. Fantastic piece of writing, penned late in preproduction by David and Dan and included in my episode. So I'm credited with writing it, but I didn't. And, of course, it's the best scene in the bloody episode.

CT: Do you have a favorite character?

BC: My favorite is Jaime. I find his arc so fascinating—watch the Jaime of the first episode and compare him to the Jaime of the finale of season four. It's an astonishing transformation. Jaime's story going forward, for me, is summed up in a line from "Oathkeeper" [season 4, Episode 404]. He's showing Brienne the White Book, where all the glorious deeds of Kingsguards past and present are recorded. Entries for other knights are full of heroics, but his small entry: shame and ignominy. He says to Brienne:

"It's the duty of the Lord Commander to fill these pages. And there's still room left on mine."

CT: Do you have a particular line or speech that is your favorite?

BC: There's an absolutely gorgeous scene between Theon Greyjoy and Maester Luwin at the close of season two ["Valar Morghulis," Episode 210], the highlight of which is Theon's tortured memory—beautifully acted by Alfie Allen—of being raised as a hostage: "You know what it's like to be told how lucky you are to be someone's prisoner? To be told how much you owe them?" I don't know if it's my favorite, but it's a great example of the empathy the show has for its most despicable characters, and Theon had been pretty despicable up to that point.

CT: Part of your role is to be on set to observe filming and advise the director when needed. Do you have a favorite moment from season four?

BC: There was one day on set I found pretty thrilling. Again, it was a "small" character moment, but that's where I think the show lives. It's a scene from the seventh episode of the season ["Mockingbird," Episode 407], where Littlefinger finally gives in to his desires and kisses Sansa in the snowy garden of the Eyrie. It's a hugely disturbing scene—mainly due to Sansa's reaction to the kiss . . .

[OPPOSITE] *The contents of* The Histories of The Lord Commanders of the Kingsguard *are accurate to the show canon and hand crafted by artist Michael Eaton.*
[ABOVE] *Jaime Lannister reviews his limited accomplishments in the White Book.*

At the start of a new season, before the production staff have returned to the office, work has already begun trying to figure out how to coordinate filming in four countries with five directors, two units, and a cast and crew of over seven hundred people. The only way to produce ten episodes a season is with very careful planning. It is down to producer Chris Newman to fit the puzzle pieces together.

CHRIS NEWMAN (PRODUCER): During season one, we had no plan to have two units on the show. But it soon became clear that having a Malta unit working in parallel to the Belfast unit was the most efficient option. The main aim is to not have an asset—a director, director of photography, or cast member—spread over two locations at once. In the beginning the only way to make things work was to instigate an episode color-coding system, cut out scene strips, and move them around on a board like chess pieces. Anyone who works in the industry knows there is no such thing as a perfect schedule. It's simply a series of distillations that you go through until you get to the one that you think is the best plan.

Generally speaking, I'll get the outline about February, and I'll spend about a month thinking about it. As a template, you try and work in episode order, but there may be a single scene in a later episode that requires a set you want to replace. You'll move that forward, if you can. You don't want to be in a situation where a director is in town for one scene and then nothing for a few weeks. We try and have a preliminary schedule early. If there are issues with build times or actor availability, the earlier we find out, the better chance we have to negotiate things like dates. Every so often you'll have an incident that will throw things off—when Kit [Harington] broke his leg, we had to push the scenes with Jon Snow back so he was able to perform his stunts—though he probably would have done them anyway if we would have let him.

[ABOVE] *Chris Newman spends much of his time on set, overseeing filming and troubleshooting.* [OPPOSITE] *An excerpt of the real schedule from Season 3. Different colors show different episodes; the first column gives the scene, the last the cast numbers.*

1.	28	EXT	Sea View, King Landing	Day	4 4/8 pgs	6, 13, 26, 51	
Stone Pier.			Sansa and Shae meet up with Little finger as she walks by the waterfront				

Raven

6	19 a	EXT	Top of the Wall	Night	5/8 pgs	8, 44, 45, 204	
Cell 4 Paint Hall			They arrive on top of the wall				

End Day # 61   Friday, September 28, 2012 -- Total Pages 10 1/8

Distant South Wolf Crew

10.	34pt	EXT	Red Keep Main Gates	Day	1/8 pgs	5, 20, 59, 100	
Pilo Gates			Jamie back at the Red Keep at last				
3.	3	EXT	King's Landing	Day	3 3/8 pgs	10, 32	
waterside gardens			Tywin quizes Pycelle on the matter of Jon Arryn's death				
6	22	EXT	Sea View, King Landing	Day	5/8 pgs	13, 26	
Stone Pier.			Sansa is too late, as Littlefingers boat sails away				

End Day # 62   Saturday, September 29, 2012 -- Total Pages 4 1/8

Distant South Wolf Crew

5.	25	EXT	Red Keep, Tyrell gardens	Day	1 7/8 pgs	13, 41, 57, 207	
Gardens			Loras and Young man temptations!				
10.	34pt	EXT	Red Keep Distant	Day	6/8 pgs	5, 20, 59, 100	
Gardens (Ruined area			Jamie back at the Red Keep at last				

End Day # 63   Sunday, September 30, 2012 -- Total Pages 2 5/8

Dragon Crew

7	2	EXT	South of the Wall	Day	2 pgs	8, 44, 45, 204	
Mourne			Wildling Raiding party now south of the wall.				
7	23	EXT	Woods (North of Winterfell)	Day	1 7/8 pgs	8, 44, 45, 204	
Mourne			Jon is tested on his knowledge of Castle Black				
7	24	EXT	Woods (North of Winterfell)	Day	3/8 pgs	8, 45	
Mourne			Deer is toasts as Jon and Ygritte hunt				

Distant South Wolf Crew

10.	2	EXT	Red Keep Gardens	Day	2 7/8 pgs	1, 13, 26, 76, 245, 248	
Gardens			Sansa and Tyrion walk in the courtyard to much amusement. They are strange allies				

10.	5	EXT	Red Keep Courtyard	Day	2 4/8 pgs	18, 26	
Ft St Lawrence			Varys encourages Shae to leave town. She declines				

End Day # 64   Monday, October 1, 2012 -- Total Pages 9 5/8

Dragon Crew

7	25	EXT	Small Cottage	Day	1 4/8 pgs	8, 45	
Mourne			Hunting and Jon and Ygritte fantazise about a life together				
8	4	EXT	Northern Hill	Day	3 3/8 pgs	8, 44, 45, 60, 204	
Mourne			Ygritte sees a tower. Jon cautions about the attack on the wall				

Distant South Wolf Crew

6	14, 15pt	EXT	Red Keep , Gardens	Day	2 pgs	13, 41	
Gardens			Sansa and Loras promenade in the Garden (also seen from High Window)				
2.	10	EXT	Red Keep Courtyard	Day	1 5/8 pgs	13, 41, 57	
Gardens (Ruined area			Loras and Sansa walk and talk				

End Day # 65   Tuesday, October 2, 2012 -- Total Pages 8 4/8

Dragon Crew

8	22pt	EXT	Harrenhall Bear Pit	Day	2 5/8 pgs	5, 20, 59, 84, 100	
Banbridge			Jamie returns for Briennne who is the days entertainment for Vargo				

Distant South Wolf Crew REST DAY

End Day # 66   Wednesday, October 3, 2012 -- Total Pages 2 5/8

Dragon Crew

8	22pt	EXT	Harrenhall Bear Pit	Day	2 2/8 pgs	5, 20, 59, 84, 100	
Banbridge			Jamie returns for Briennne who is the days entertainment for Vargo				

Distant South Wolf Crew

2.	11	EXT	Red Keep Gardens	Day	4 7/8 pgs	13, 56, 57, 239	
Gardens			Oleanna Tyrell extracts from Sansa her true opinion of Joffrey				

End Day # 67   Thursday, October 4, 2012 -- Total Pages 7 1/8

Belfast Dragon Crew

9.	4	INT	Twins Audience Room	Day	4 pgs	2, 9, 54, 58, 77, 90, 96, 97, 210, 244	
B Stage Paint Hall			Robb and Mother are apologising to Walder and all his daughters				

— FINDING WESTEROS —

From the cliffs at Dragonstone to the battlefields of the Riverlands and even beyond the Wall, Northern Ireland has provided a huge portion of the locations seen on Game of Thrones. *Locations manager Robbie Boake is responsible for finding Westeros in the real world, including King's Landing in Armagh and Castle Black in Larne.*

ROBBIE BOAKE (LOCATIONS MANAGER): Initially, I'll look at the outline when it comes out and break down what I feel will be on an interior set or in another country, things we can't replicate here. I will generally have about a month to scout as much as I can. Finding the actual locations is all legwork. I drive around for hours and hike up hills and through forests.

At that point the producer's scouts will begin. It's true that on *Game of Thrones* you have a single designer, but unlike a film we have multiple directors who may all have different ideas. As the scripts evolve, the options for suitable locations will naturally reduce. They are going in with a clear idea of what direction characters are going to be traveling from or how a stunt might play out. Once you are into that detail, you begin to look at the logistical elements—do fences need to be taken down, or are there houses visible that need to be screened off? Is there an area for unit base within a manageable distance of set, and can any animals manage the terrain?

Soon you reach this stage where a multitude of other departments become involved: construction could be building sets, SFX could be smoking an area up or snowing it up. Then we need to secure government permissions. In a public area, safety and security is always the main concern. We want to protect the intellectual property of the show until airing and maintain the mythology of the show. It's not as magical if you can see a set looking like a set in the middle of some beautiful countryside. On private land, it's incredibly important that people don't trespass in order to find a set.

We endeavor to leave every location we use as we found it, and in many cases in better condition—we'll do repairs to roads to improve access or buildings for safety. We want to be able to continue filming, particularly at locations we may want to revisit—not everyone realizes how many places like Shane's Castle have been used repeatedly. From the first moment it became the Winterfell crypt, and it has since been reused as many dungeons. It's been Ned Stark's cell, a Dragonstone cell, and even part of the Twins receiving room. This season, Shane's will also play host to the Red Keep Forge. The grounds have hosted well over twenty scenes, ranging from the tourney grounds in season one to some of Theon's most recent scenes. Cairn Castle also has hosted a huge number of key scenes, from the first execution in Episode 101 to Ygritte shooting Jon, as well as playing host to the King's Road and all the parties that travel upon it.

[ABOVE] *Ballintoy is mostly known for the Iron Islands harbour, but the beach on the other side of the track plays home to Dragonstone.* [OPPOSITE] *The show films in multiple locations across Northern Ireland, often in extremely remote locations with difficult logistics.*

WRITING THE THEME
— INTERVIEW WITH RAMIN DJAWADI —

Game of Thrones *composer Ramin Djawadi studied film music at the Berkley College of Music in Boston before moving to Los Angeles to work with Oscar-winning composer Hans Zimmer at Remote Control Productions. He became involved with* Game of Thrones *after being approached by David Benioff and Dan Weiss, who showed him the first two episodes and a rough cut of the title sequence. Ramin has been working on the music of the show since the pilot.*

C. A. TAYLOR: How did it all begin for you?

RAMIN DJAWADI (COMPOSER): The guys were incredibly smart—they sent me over to watch this rough cut of the titles and showed me what they had been working on. I was so inspired by the strength of the visuals I started working on it straight away.

CT: When it comes to composing a soundtrack or theme, is the story more important or the visuals?

RD: To be honest, it's a combination of the two. I always find it amazing: when I read the script or hear the story, I have certain expectations, and then when you see the acting and the sets, it can alter that. Even when I am not writing specifically to a scene, I tend to have the visuals on in the background to help immerse myself in the world.

CT: Costume designer Michele Clapton says she often thinks of characters as certain colors when she is designing their costumes. Are there instruments that represent people to you?

RD: Definitely. Part of the way I see notes is in color, so if there is a particular visual that is red or yellow, certain keys or notes come out. This show is quite challenging. One of the first things David, Dan, and I talked about was how complex and layered the story was and how the characters were organized. How could we best lay these themes out? I like to use Daenerys as an example—when the story first started out, you had no idea how powerful she was going to become. It was very important to create a theme for a certain character or houses that could be turned into something powerful, dark, or sad. The theme had to have those elements implanted early without necessarily hearing them all immediately. "The Rains of Castamere" is another good example—from the beginning you knew it was being set up to be the big Red Wedding piece. It was both fun and challenging, and we watched it evolve to get to that place.

CT: Looking back, are there any particular pieces or character themes that stand out as favorites?

RD: One of the ones I have recently finished, "Mhysa," remains a favorite. Again, it is a wonderful Daenerys moment. That track has a female choir, a male choir, and even a children's choir all singing these lyrics—a very powerful track.

Also, the love theme for Jon Snow and Ygritte when they finally make it up and over the Wall—I thought that was quite a powerful piece, and I was very happy with the way it turned out. Sometimes it's the case of blending two individual themes, but we don't always have single themes—sometimes there is a theme for a particular storyline or location, or a character only gets a theme depending on how prevalent the story is. Theon was like that—he only got a theme in season two.

CT: When you go to the studio, do you always work with live musicians?

RD: Live musicians provide a character and depth that I feel can't really be replicated with a computer. If I have any choice, it's always my preference to work with them. It raises the quality of the work. Having said that, there are moments where I have used synthesizers layered into the sound because in those instances they fit into *Game of Thrones.*

CT: Do the different worlds add to the challenge or the fun of *Game of Thrones?* The contrast of the hot and sultry Essos to the ethereal wasteland North of the Wall, for example.

RD: Definitely the fun of it. Taking Daenerys: We do have more Eastern influences with her, like the bedug [an Indonesian hanging drum], whereas North of the Wall I use glass bowls to create the feeling of iciness. Again, this is where the visuals are so important. You see Daenerys surrounded by desert or the Night's Watch in a landscape of empty color—it's a lot of fun to paint that with music. We hear about the White Walkers before we ever really see them, but underneath there is still a mild echo giving the scene a depth and resonance that should make you a little afraid.

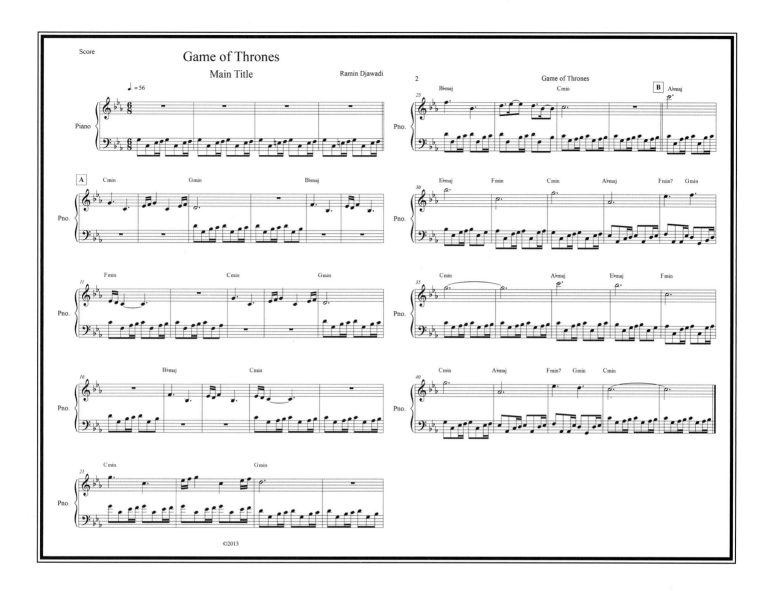

CT: How do you approach a visceral scene like the Red Wedding, and a song like "The Rains of Castamere," which are so pivotal for the show?

RD: The season before, we'd started to discuss what this scene needed to be: beautiful, haunting, and so on. I'd already been leading up to it with the Lannisters in season two. In a way, by the time we got to the wedding, there was a sense of what was to come when the music began. I think that's why perhaps it had the effect it did, subconsciously.

CT: Do you look at particular historical references when composing, such as for a bawdy house song like "The Bear and the Maiden Fair"?

RD: I try not to. I try to just go for it because of the beauty and scope of the fantasy world we are in. It isn't a historical piece, so I don't have to think in terms of baroque or Renaissance influences. But instead: How far can I take something without it being totally out of place? I'd argue you could play "The Bear" on the acoustic guitar, if you wanted to.

CT: The Game of Thrones title sequence is arguably one of the most identifiable themes of recent years. How do you feel about the reaction to it?

RD: Somehow everything seems to work. There was a definite connection between the visuals and the music. I remember the day after it first aired, David and Dan sent me a link to a YouTube video of someone playing the music on a different instrument. Then all the different videos started rolling in, and I was just blown away. It was amazing to see people playing their own versions on accordions, recorders, flute, and electric guitars. One video that impressed me the most was someone who had hooked up all these electronic hard drives and had them playing the theme. I don't even know how they did that! It was incredible.

[ABOVE] *Sheet music for the title music of* **Game of Thrones**.

— CREATING THE TITLE SEQUENCE —

Each episode of Game of Thrones *begins with the Emmy Award–winning title sequence, which has become such an instantly recognizable signature of the show. The brainchild of the creative team at Elastic in Los Angeles, the title sequence contains so many details that it is easy to miss them on first viewing—from the individual coats of arms alongside the producer credits to the sigils emblazoned on the Da Vinci–inspired models that unfurl from the map. Ultimately, the title sequence tells a story of its own that evolves along with the series.*

ANGUS WALL (CREATIVE DIRECTOR): After the pilot was filmed, some people were confused by the geography, so we started playing with the idea of maps. Initially, the visuals were cut into the show between scenes, which was effective but really broke up the narrative. We were struggling with what the concept was to be and then we decided to create what you might find inside a fantasy book cover with maps and a key. Dan and David had written the title sequence as a crow's flight from King's Landing to Winterfell, but it seemed quite flat. We wanted to create a version of the world that was really easy to understand using 3-D models, and very quickly we realized that it made the most sense to put these models within a sphere, a closed environment, because you would be able to see what was coming. If you were on the outside of a sphere, these elements would be hidden behind the horizon. It was a huge leap forward to invert the world.

One of the early type studies was titled Mad Monk, as we were using Ralph Steadman's gestural type as a general inspiration. Somehow, the idea stuck and became this concept of these mad monks, somewhere in the world of the series, watching the events unfolding and perhaps even influencing them in some way.

HAMEED SHAUKAT (PRODUCER): As the world changes, they update the map. For instance, Harrenhal was once a mighty fortress that was then destroyed. In our map, Harrenhal is inert. It remains the only site that doesn't animate, as it's "broken."

KIRK SHINTANI (CG SUPERVISOR): The map is supposed to be a living version of the world, so when Winterfell burns, it is also laid waste on the map and appears destroyed.

ANGUS WALL (CREATIVE DIRECTOR): Bringing in new cities definitely keeps it interesting. The title sequence is actually different depending on the episode, telling you each of the locations you will travel within the episode. Obviously, some episodes mimic the same path, but generally you have about three or four different sequences per season. By the end of season four, we will have completed fourteen different versions of the titles.

ANGUS WALL (CREATIVE DIRECTOR): Our job is basically to play the part of the monks maintaining the map.

HAMEED SHAUKAT (PRODUCER): There are no real hidden elements, but there is a lot of detail. When you pull back to bands on the astrolabe, you see these intricate motifs. If you know what you are looking for, you will see that they tell the story of the fall of the Targaryen Dynasty, starting in Valyria and ending with the rise of Robert Baratheon. Some people have found this, of course, but they aren't spelled out for you. We have also tried to incorporate the sigils of the reigning families at each location, so the Baratheon sigil is in King's Landing, the Starks were at Winterfell, and this season we have included the flayed man at the Dreadfort for the Boltons. We even had the Horse Gates at Vaes Dothrak. The only element that no one seems to have seen yet is that the Fist of the First Men is labeled and just barely visible on the map above the Wall.

KIRK SHINTANI (CG SUPERVISOR): We went into season one with the idea that the gears and cogs would function together, to move up and down, to make the models behave correctly. This also goes back to an earlier idea that everything could be made with a hammer, saw, and chisel.

ANGUS WALL (CREATIVE DIRECTOR): We start with the descriptions in the books, but we also bring in the concept art from the show. We have an incredibly talented artist, Rustam Hasanov, who spends a good deal of time looking at all the references in the books when he is putting together the concepts—is it a rich city, a poor one? Is it a trade city or a slave one?

HAMEED SHAUKAT (PRODUCER): Sometimes the CG team takes creative license, but this can be necessary. Take Dragonstone: On the show you only ever see it from the beach. We needed a whole city with an aerial view, so knowing things like it needs to be in the shape of a dragon and that it was the Targaryen seat allows the CG team to take the creative licence it needs to make things wholly recognizable, yet allow for interpretation. In our sequence, the first angle you see of Dragonstone mimics what you see from the beach, so it doesn't seem out of place to the viewer.

HAMEED SHAUKAT (PRODUCER): When it came to the music, composer Ramin Djawadi came to see the sequence. He walked around the studio and saw all the concepts and the different elements, and then he went away to work on it. He came back around three days later with the finished theme. It was genuinely one of the most impressive turnarounds that I have experienced.

HAMEED SHAUKAT (PRODUCER): All credit has to go to the team we worked with in season one, in addition to us and [Art Director] Rob Feng we had a team of twenty-seven people working on this title sequence. That includes everyone from compositors to the CG team and if we have a streamlined process now, it's only because of the foundations that were created then.

[OPPOSITE] *Concept art showing the detailing of the Astrolabe blades.* [ABOVE] *Close up of the mechanical towers that grow into King's Landing, designed by Elastic.*

— CREATING VALYRIAN —

In the world of Game of Thrones, *High Valyrian is an ancient language from the Valyrian Freehold. At one stage the Valyrians held an empire that encompassed massive swathes of land. As a result, a version of the language known as "Low" Valyrian is still spoken in the region and in the nine Free Cities to the West (though each has its own distinct dialect and linguistic evolutions).*

The use of High Valyrian is now mainly limited to the clergy and the gentry, making Daenerys's fluency a surprising but useful strategic tool. Unlike Dothraki, the vocabulary created for the books was limited to a handful of words and phrases, making its realization an exciting challenge for linguist David J. Peterson.

GEORGE R. R. MARTIN (CO-EXECUTIVE PRODUCER AND AUTHOR): I really have to give David Peterson 95 percent of the credit on the languages. Tolkien was a world-class linguist, and even before he was writing *Lord of the Rings*, he created not one but two elvish languages. He also created the language of the dwarves, Westernesse, and Númenor—he loved creating fantasy languages. His true heir, in that sense, is absolutely David Peterson.

I'm not a linguist. I don't speak Old Norse or Old English the way that Tolkien did. When my books go out internationally, I rely on translators. For me it's like a conjurer's trick—I create a few words and try and give it a particular flavor. Then I just write the line and add "Daenerys said in High Valyrian." Of course, you can't do that on a show. I used to get letters, before the show came out, from language enthusiasts who were asking about vocabulary and syntax for High Valyrian. I'd have to write back and say, "Sorry, fella, I've only invented seven words of it, and when I need an eighth, I'll come up with that."

This is definitely a case of the show picking up the ball and running with it far further than I would have been able to go.

DAVID J. PETERSON (LINGUIST): In much the same way as I began with the Dothraki language, my first step with Valyrian was to pull all the words George [R. R. Martin] had created from the texts. This took much less time than with Dothraki because, other than *valar morghulis, valar dohaeris,* and the words for "little brother," there were really only a few stray ones. Anyone who has read the books knows how memorable and strong they are as phrases, so it didn't take long to gather them. I didn't want to start with *valar morghulis,* as that would take us into the complexities of all the grammar. I knew that George wanted High Valyrian to inhabit the same place in their society that Latin does in ours. Aside from that, I tried to collect all the names that were either definitely Valyrian or looked Valyrian in shape.

The names proved to be quite useful. In fact, I started with the names, broke down all the common endings of each of them, and used them to work out all the noun classifications with a certain number of fixated endings. From that I was able to generate a gender system, but unlike Latin with just masculine, feminine, and neuter, I decided to do something a bit more fun. Based originally on an older split between animate and inanimate nouns, where both came in two varieties, I created a four-gender system, which became the solar, lunar, terrestrial, and aquatic genders. Certain characteristic nouns that fall into those classifications—like some of the more common irregular nouns, like in *solar* the word for sun and in *lunar* the word for moon—those became the paradigms for those genders. That starting point was definitely where the most help came from the books.

In effect, there are actually *two* versions of High Valyrian. There are people who still speak it, like Daenerys, but she doesn't quite pronounce it the way that they would have back when it was the actual language. In fact, it almost exists grammatically closer to the old language than it would have in the Valyrian Freehold before the destruction. Back then, they would have just been speaking the language, and it would have changed and evolved. The idea is that the Targaryen line wanted to keep the language pure, so they would have kept away from changes that other Valyrian lines would have been using so it's not grammatically altered. At the same time it doesn't reflect the reality of the language as it would have been. She's effectively representing a snapshot of a destroyed empire.

In contrast, the radical changes that you see in Low Valyrian in particular are the ones you hear spoken in and around Slaver's Bay. They can all understand each other, though the language of Yunkai and Astapor are much closer to each other than to the language of Meereen. The comparison would perhaps be the difference between someone speaking with a thick Scottish accent compared to someone from New England. For Daenerys, the language in Meereen would be near impenetrable; it's just too different. I had a lot of fun creating both the original language and the descendant version, one that would be related in the same way that Latin would be to Spanish. It's not something we've really ever had a chance to see before. If you look at Tolkien's work, we never saw the most ancient versions of the language in the actual books, only the descendants.

JACOB ANDERSON (GREY WORM): At the start it seemed almost impossible. I remember looking at the first email from David Peterson with MP3s, thinking, "How am I going to do this?" In the beginning I thought I could maybe just copy what he was saying, but I quickly realized that was not going to work. You have to know what he's saying, and I wanted to know what he was saying. It's another challenge again to work out what each word means, what the vowel sounds are, where the emphasis is. It's the biggest challenge I've had, but it's *fun.*

DAVID J. PETERSON (LINGUIST): Jacob Anderson is without a doubt the best performer I have ever seen when it comes to working with a created language. Literally, of everything I have seen or worked on, he is the best I have ever come across. I was also really taken by Emilia Clarke, who did such an amazing job with the intonations. This is a language that has a very distinct rhythm that is quite different from Dothraki, and she just nails it. The way she puts it together, it sounds like full sentences and clauses and in precisely the right way. That's the main thing the actor has to do with a created language to really sell it.

[OPPOSITE] *Daenerys is one of the few living speakers of High Valyrian.*

SEASO

N III

Part One

BEYOND THE WALL

"If we don't make it, if we don't warn them down in the kingdoms, before winter's done, everyone you've ever known will be dead."

— LORD COMMANDER JEOR MORMONT

THE LAND OF WESTEROS IS IN UPHEAVAL. NORTH OF THE WALL, JON SNOW IS ON A MISSION TO MEET THE MYSTERIOUS MANCE RAYDER, LEADER OF THE HUGE WILDLING ARMY. AT THE SAME TIME, SNOW'S COMRADE ON THE NIGHT'S WATCH, SAMWELL TARLY, IS TRYING TO RETURN TO THE WALL WITH SEPARATE NEWS THAT COULD CHANGE EVERYTHING: THE LEGENDARY, HORRIFIC WHITE WALKERS NOT ONLY EXIST BUT ARE MOVING SOUTH AS WELL.

UNBEKNOWNST TO JON, HIS TWO YOUNGEST BROTHERS ARE TRAVELING NORTH WITH THE GENTLE GIANT HODOR AND THE EVER-LOYAL OSHA. THEY FIND THEMSELVES FOLLOWING BRAN'S DREAM VISIONS AND GUIDED BY THEIR MYSTERIOUS NEW COMPANIONS, MEERA AND JOJEN REED, WHO HAVE MORE TO SHOW BRAN THAN THE DIRECTION.

THE WILDLINGS:
A BRIEF HISTORY

"WE DON'T CALL OURSELVES WILDLINGS, WE CALL OURSELVES FREE FOLK. WE DON'T BOW DOWN TO PERFUMED LORDLINGS WHOSE GREAT-GRANDDADDIES WON SOME BATTLE NO ONE CAN REMEMBER NO MORE."

— CRASTER

THOUSANDS OF YEARS AGO, WHEN BRAN THE BUILDER BEGAN THE CONSTRUCTION OF THE WALL, he divided more than a country. He forever divided the people. North of the Wall, without rule of either sovereign or lord, the tribes and clans known as the free folk remained, and they have continued to survive, living in numbers without record.

Predated only by the mysterious Children of the Forest and descended from the First Men, they have lived in Westeros thousands of years longer than the southern kings, who arrived with the invasion of the Andals, a mere sixty-five hundred years earlier. As such, the free folk take great pride in their freedom, and they do not recognize the claims of sovereignty from south of the Wall—indeed, they do not kneel to anyone, and they follow only their own chosen leaders.

Elsewhere, the free folk are known derogatively as the wildlings. Many consider them to be crude and ill-educated, almost savages. Despite their border raids beyond the Wall and skirmishes with the Night's Watch, the wildlings pose little threat to the kingdoms of northern Westeros, with whom they have maintained an ancient feud. Their scattered, primitive society isn't seen as a cause for real concern.

Now, though, a new winter is coming, and the wildling clans have gathered together to create an overwhelming force, led by a mysterious "King-beyond-the-Wall," a deserter from the Night's Watch and a legendary ranger: Mance Rayder.

[PREVIOUS SPREAD] *Jon Snow trades his black cloak for wildling furs.* [OPPOSITE] *Ygritte (Rose Leslie) travels with a wildling party.* [ABOVE] *Rattleshirt (Edward Dogliani) stands guard in Mance Rayder's wildling camp.*

MANCE RAYDER

"DO YOU KNOW HOW I GOT MOON WORSHIPPERS AND CANNIBALS AND GIANTS TO MARCH TOGETHER, IN THE SAME ARMY? I TOLD THEM WE'RE ALL GOING TO DIE IF WE DON'T GET SOUTH."

—MANCE RAYDER TO JON SNOW

Mance Rayder (Ciarán Hinds) was originally a member of the Night's Watch who was wounded by a shadow cat attack during a patrol in the Skirling Pass. Mance was taken to a wildling village for healing, and his shredded cloak was mended by a wise woman using scarlet silk—a great treasure for her and a generous gift to bestow on a ranger. However, when Mance returned to the Wall, his repaired cloak, shot through with red, was taken from him, for it was no longer the black he had sworn to wear. As the sun rose the next day,

Mance left the Wall, and the Night's Watch, and headed north—all for the freedom to choose his own cloak.

Now, in the land that stretches out beyond the shadow of the Wall, he has become a leader of the wildlings. Mance is bringing the warring tribes and isolated clans together with a single purpose: to survive the fast-approaching winter, and the deathless walking nightmares that are arriving with it, by crossing the Wall—perhaps the only thing that can withstand their relentless onslaught.

CIARÁN HINDS (MANCE RAYDER): The scale of *Game of Thrones* continues to get grander and wider. It's an epic world, so heavily influenced by alliances and treaties. Everyone in it has a nature, be it good or bad, driven by every motivation, from fear and lust to power and greed. There's a mystery I appreciate. There are no guarantees where anyone is going to end up.

I think the wildling people needed someone to lead, and Mance is the most gifted among them. I don't think he considers himself king. He believes in the idea that the wildlings do not kneel. Right now he's driven by pure desperation. All of these people are in danger of being wiped out. He knows it will lead to a fight, but in his mind it's simple: we're coming over no matter what—because what's out there, behind us, is worse.

KIT HARINGTON (JON SNOW): Having watched Ciarán in countless stage performances, I feel like he is one of our greatest living actors. He has such an intense stare. Those fantastically crazy eyes are perfect for Mance. I think Jon Snow utterly respects Mance. He knows this guy is incredibly clever and charismatic, enigmatic even. There's an element of hero worship, but their meeting isn't clear-cut. Mance even says so to Jon. I think Mance does want the power now that he's got it, and Jon is worried about what will happen if they do all end up south of the Wall. Jon can't forget about the thousands of years of tension and conflict between the wildlings and the northmen just because of one man's words.

[ABOVE] *Mance greets Jon Snow.* [OPPOSITE] *Mance Rayder played by Ciarán Hinds.*

— BUILDING MANCE'S CAMP —

On a lava field near Mývatn, Iceland, production designer Gemma Jackson and her production team needed just under a month to create Mance's camp, as they battled the thick snows of an Icelandic winter. However, the main tent that is the focus of the wildlings' camp was first built four months before in Belfast at the Paint Hall studio and was the setting for the first scene between Mance and Jon. After this single scene was filmed, the main tent was then deconstructed and moved to Iceland for on-location scenes.

Art director Ashleigh Jeffers designed the look of the wildling camp with the idea that the area would be devoid of building supplies. All structures would have been created out of salvaged or hunted materials, such as mammoth or whale bone. The wildlings are transient and on the move, and Mance's camp would need to be packed and carried through the snow.

Evoking a rib cage, the skeleton of the main tent was made from carved pieces of polystyrene, which were layered with plaster to create the smooth shape and width of the bones. Each "rib" was then painted and aged to reflect the weathering of such an extreme climate. Making the bones took five weeks, and it took a further two weeks to put up the frame and dress it with the animal-hide walls, pieced together from a mix of different animal skins.

Once in Iceland, Ashleigh worked with the local crew to recreate Mance's tent and the village around it. However, not all the tents you see on screen are real. To reflect the size of Mance's following in wider shots, the VFX department replicated and extended the number of tents, showing the village fading out in the distance.

ASHLEIGH JEFFERS (ART DIRECTOR): The process of the build in Iceland was no different from the construction in Belfast, except for the fact we were battling the weather. The first week there, we were stuck in the hotel—it was a complete white-out with snow drifts eight feet up the windows. We had to call in diggers to excavate the roads through fifteen feet of snow. The crevasses on the lava field were hidden, and the rocks were brutally sharp. We lost one of the vehicles in one of the hidden valleys one day, but we loved all that adventure.

In the end, we got the structure up in a day, then the skins on the next day. We had to—if we had left it half covered, it would have acted as a sail and been ripped away by the strong winds. We had it lashed down with fishing nets that held it together. When the weather did come in, the snow and ice actually acted as our cement to hold it down. The main challenge was keeping it up until the shooting crew arrived and then clearing the snow. Ironically, when we laid the horse carcass set down a few hundred feet away, we lost all the snow. It melted and we had to bring more in—both fake and from a nearby drift.

[OPPOSITE] *Concept design for Mance's Camp.* [TOP] *Icelandic extras prepare for a take.*
[ABOVE] *Marks are laid down for Jon Snow's entrance to camp.*

— FILMING IN ICELAND —

Game of Thrones *has filmed in Iceland since season two, and the country has provided some of the most dramatic settings on the show. The original choice of Iceland was in no little part due to producer Chris Newman, who previously had both lived and worked in Iceland. In seasons three and four, the island was featured even more. The different landscapes within its shores provide ideal settings for the extreme lands beyond the Wall and, during summer, for the dramatic hills and valleys of the Vale. In all,* Game of Thrones *has so far filmed in seventeen separate Icelandic locations, including in national parks and on glaciers, up mountains and by thermal power stations, and even in lava fields. Despite occasionally being trapped in snowed-in hotels and having trucks buried by blizzards, all anyone ever says about shooting there is how much they love the people and the incredible landscape.*

CHRIS NEWMAN (PRODUCER): If money were no object, you might consider filming in New Zealand in the winter, but it might not be the best use of funds. The alternative is to try to create something, but there is a limit to how much you can mock up to look like snow. After a few years you start to worry that things look fatigued on dressed sets. In Iceland, you can always find permanent snow—even if it's icy and on a glacier—and still have good access by road.

Going to Iceland is not like traveling to a country with no infrastructure. Their economy includes sport tourism. We weren't creating a filming structure in a totally alien environment. Plus, I knew the local crew could handle an indigenous shoot: filming Icelandic scenes with Icelandic crew. That's the best way to go about it.

There are challenges. The journey times can be long and there are limitations to what you can do. You want to limit the number of actors, for example. You have to think about the amount of equipment you can actually get into each location. Then, you tend to use the landscape as a backdrop or canvas for intimate scenes,

letting the scenery seep into the shot more organically. With large action sequences, you can sometimes lose the background to weather. You have to consider the available filming hours, too. If you have only five and a half hours in a day, you need to take setup times into account. Can you access the areas in the dark, and is it safe to do so?

You don't want scenes to look contrived. You want it to be believable that characters would stop and chat in a particular location. Filming in these locations helps the actors, too: You don't have to act being cold. No one has to remind you to shiver.

A bonus is, of course, that local Viking societies can provide the perfect look for our wildling and Night's Watch extras. The people of Iceland seem to enjoy having us there almost as much as we enjoy going there.

[OPPOSITE (TOP)] *Mance Rayder and Jon Snow talk while traveling south.* [OPPOSITE (BOTTOM)] *In the Icelandic snow, the stunt team prepares to attack Samwell Tarly as he runs from the army of wights in the opening scene of season three.* [ABOVE] *Extras begin their march into the snowdrifts of Iceland.*

— COSTUMING THE WILDLINGS —

When costume designer Michele Clapton first considered clothing for the wildlings, she wanted to create looks that subtly distinguished a variety of peoples. The lands beyond the Wall are very expansive, and this would naturally lead to societal differences. Wildlings near the coasts would have armor shirts made from oysters or mussel shells, while those farther inland might have furs or, like Rattleshirt, might adorn their clothes with bones.

Wildling clothes would also be hand sewn. To mimic this, different types of hide are held together with latex thonging to make them appear lashed together. The toggles that work as closings are shaped to look like bone, but in reality these are cast and painted plastic. To make a single jacket takes half a day. Seamstresses use a ten-inch mattress needle to stitch the leathers together, protecting their hands with the same handguards sailors use when mending sails. Prepunching the hides could give the appearance of manufacture,

which Michele is determined to avoid. The average jacket weighs approximately 8½ pounds, while the heaviest are nearly 17½ pounds, and that's before the shells and bones are even added.

Each wildling coat is also hand painted with images similar to cave paintings, of mammoths and creatures that roam the icy lands. Headdresses and hats are made as organically as possible, with weaving and knotting to create the impression that they were fashioned out of materials found in the wild. Crampon-style blades made out of deer antlers, which wildlings could strap on their feet, are the ultimate winter accessory.

To armorer Tommy Dunne, the variety of wildlings also means a variety of weapons. Some would be deserters of the Watch, like Mance, who would have brought their own swords or knives, but even these would need to be adapted and shortened.

TOMMY DUNNE (ARMORER): In five-foot snowdrifts it would be impossible to have a thirty-two-inch blade. As you drag it, it would just become an ice block and get heavier. I also thought of the wildlings more as a guerrilla force, attacking and moving on quickly, so we didn't worry about the larger weapons used for sieges. I wanted to think of it as a return to nature, living off the land and the animals they hunt. Realistically, there would be very limited access to wood, so I looked at using antlers and bone for handles and weapons. We do use real bone, but only those antlers that are naturally dropped by the herd each year. We are lucky to have a good supply.

[OPPOSITE] *Hand-painted wildling costume.* [ABOVE] *Antler made crampons for ice-walking.* [RIGHT] *Intricate designs on the original design for Ygritte's costume.* [FOLLOWING SPREAD] *Concept art showing the scale of the Wall before Sam and Gilly attempt the climb.*

— THE WALL —
EPISODE 306: "THE CLIMB"

Built forty-five hundred years ago, the Wall is one of the most significant structures in Westeros. Standing around seven hundred to eight hundred feet tall and covering more than three hundred miles, the Wall was constructed to defend Westeros against the secret terrors of the North, the White Walkers, now long forgotten and turned into legend. As this happened, the Wall was slowly abandoned and let fall into ruin. Of the original nineteen castles along the Wall, only three are still manned: the Shadow Tower, Eastwatch-by-the-Sea, and Castle Black. It remains, however, a daunting obstacle. In Episode 306, Mance and his wildling army travel toward the Wall, and Mance orders a small party to scale the Wall in preparation for his attack. This dramatic scene became one of the largest production challenges of season three.

ALIK SAKHAROV (DIRECTOR): It was very important that there was a sense that it was a continuous forward climb. When I first storyboarded the scene, I had about eighty VFX shots—too many by far. I wanted to see the abyss below and the vast empty sky as they climbed. It became clear quickly that I couldn't work it that way. Then it became very subjective—it was all about the interactions of the characters. Words aren't spoken, but you sense the tension. The most important thing for me was that we didn't pull the actors up the Wall. Instead, they had to climb it. We needed to see the exertion and the effort in order to sell it. The Wall had to have the space to accommodate all four climbers at once, so they were really all climbing together.

TOM MARTIN (CONSTRUCTION MANAGER): In the beginning we did tests on the look—some people thought it should be like a glacier; others wanted compacted snow and ice, as the Wall was supposed to be man-made. Once [production designer] Gemma Jackson agreed on the style, we built a basic timber frame and coated it in scrim and plaster for the foundation and to build up the shape. Then we sprayed on hot wax and handfuls of sea salt to create the look of crystallization. In the stunt tests it quickly became clear this was too thin. The test climbers were sometimes striking through to the timber frame. In the end, we completely changed the process. We did a full polystyrene sculpt with the plaster and wax, and as it was curing, we blew in

small amounts of glitter to give it a snowlike shimmer. One of the best things was accidental: the salt crystals absorbed water and formed frozen droplets in the cool temperatures of the vast interior of the Paint Hall in winter, which actually made the surface cool to the touch for the climbers.

During filming, we had a team of four ready to fix any immediate damage between takes, using blowtorches and a compound of wax and SFX powder snow to patch the wall. Overnight, for the whole three-week shoot, we had two teams who would start from the bottom and refinish the entire wall, so that each morning the climbers could start on a new fresh wall set. From start to finish, including all the tests for VFX, SFX, and stunts, the Wall remains one of the longest set builds on the show, taking about twelve weeks to complete.

KIT HARINGTON (JON SNOW): It was a grueling shoot. They left you a little slack in the harness line, just enough so you really had to climb, and if you slipped, you would drop. At one point I was strapped to the Wall from behind and hauling Rose [Leslie, who plays the wildling Ygritte] up while facing forward, and it felt like you could fall all this way while you looked down. It wasn't eight hundred feet, but it helped you imagine it. Of

[OPPOSITE] *Wall climb concept art.* [ABOVE] *Green screen tests in Paint Hall Cell 4.*

course, Rose did have to drop when the Wall gave way, and she was amazing. For the bigger stuff, the stunt people came in. What's amazing is the way they watch your performance and mimic your style, how you move and climb and even how you use your axe. In the end, it was a wonderful dance to work with them.

ROSE LESLIE (YGRITTE): You had to believe it. You wanted to see the strain in the face, the grip of the hand. As an actor, you want that depth in your performance. You could be hanging out in your harness for long periods of time, but just before filming, we turned over, and they would give you just enough slack so that you were on the Wall with your full weight. We had a wind machine from one side, and snow coming in from the other. For the four of us it was very real. You felt you were right on the Wall. Alik would remind us on each take of the threat of making a wrong move and what that could mean.

JOE BAUER (VFX SUPERVISOR): An awful lot of care was given to the real set by the art department. The need to have four people climbing at once really dictated its size. We had two main sequences, one at two hundred feet and one at five hundred feet,

which were mainly differentiated by the weather. At the lower altitude, it's cloudy and the beginnings of a storm are brewing. But we also wanted to create a feeling of "Look how high we are"—as an audience, we have never been so high. By the time they reach the upper sequence, the characters are almost ripped off the Wall by the force of the storm.

VFX extended and expanded the horizons, creating our own Wall of China, essentially. We started by fully scanning the actual set so we had a 3-D computer model to work from and could use that for tracking. The top of the Wall is very different, of course. It's a tiny set in real life, and the actors had to bunch together. When they get there, it's the first time we see that kind of view. We used two matte painters to create the view of what they had left behind and used that as a base. Then we used a photograph of a location in Southern Ireland to create the epic vista of the South—what they are moving toward. We lit it in a romantic light, since it's a significant moment for Jon and Ygritte. It's the moment they fall in love—we wanted the view to represent the possibilities that holds.

[ABOVE] *Tormund leads the climb.* [OPPOSITE] *Jon Snow and Ygritte reach the top alive.*

JOJEN REED

"WE'VE COME A LONG WAY TO FIND YOU, BRANDON.
AND WE HAVE MUCH FARTHER TO GO."

—JOJEN REED

Jojen Reed (Thomas Brodie-Sangster) first appeared as a mysterious boy in a dream of Bran's when Bran was trying to track and kill the Three-Eyed Raven. When he was a small boy, Jojen was struck down by a fever that seemed as if it would take his life. His sister, Meera, nursed him for ten nights until the fever broke. When he awoke, he had the sight—but the visions take a toll on his still-fragile body in the form of violent seizures. Jojen has some knowledge of the warg, or someone who has the ability to enter and take control of an animal and make use of its senses. Jojen believes his visions are guiding him to take Bran north of the Wall to find the real Three-Eyed Raven that follows them both in their dreams.

THOMAS BRODIE-SANGSTER (JOJEN REED): I saw Jojen as someone different from everyone that Bran had ever met before. I like playing on the idea that at the beginning the audience had no idea if Jojen and Meera are good or bad. Jojen is so young and with such strong powers—he can be very intimidating.

He's grown up with the sight. It's part of who he is. He is someone who sees it as a burden as much as a gift, but he is very accepting of it. He is, in fact, very accepting of everyone and the choices they make in life. He's a very selfless character—he's not driven by greed or power, but simply by his faith in his visions. In my mind, he is one of the most level-headed of all the people on the show because of it.

[ABOVE] *Jojen Reed played by Thomas Brodie-Sangster.*
[OPPOSITE] *Meera Reed played by Ellie Kendrick.*

MEERA REED

"SOME PEOPLE WILL ALWAYS NEED HELP. THAT DOESN'T MEAN
THEY AREN'T WORTH HELPING."

—MEERA REED

Howland Reed once saved Ned Stark's life, and he was one of Ned's closest allies and friends during Robert's Rebellion. Now Howland's children, Jojen and Meera, are bound by fate with Ned's son Bran. Led to Bran by Jojen's visions, Meera Reed (Ellie Kendrick) uses her skills to hunt for food and, above all, to protect her brother. When Meera first meets Bran's protectress, Osha (Natalia Tena), she manages to get the upper hand on the woman, and they continue to struggle to find common ground. Eventually, when the group is forced to part ways, Osha must trust that Meera will work equally hard to protect Bran as well.

ELLIE KENDRICK (MEERA REED): Their motivations are quite pure—for Meera, she just wants to protect her brother so he can follow his vision. They don't care about power or politics. It's about loyalty. I liked the fact their characters turn a cliché on its head—it's a girl who does all the fighting to protect a boy. Meera is very level-headed. She's open and honest. It's a joy to play a strong woman who isn't a bitch. There are so few. I knew the books and had always been drawn to the strong tomboy characters like Arya, so I was excited to get a chance to do stunts and learn skills.

OSHA

"I LEARNED HOW TO WALK IN DARKNESS."

—OSHA, ON LEAVING BRAN

Osha (Natalia Tena) is a wildling woman from north of the Wall. She was once living with a man who disappeared. Though others in the village said he'd left her, she didn't believe it. Sadly, she was proven right when, late one night, he did return—but as an undead wight, with unnaturally blue eyes the color of the sky. As the thing that was once her lover attacked, she plunged a knife deep into its heart, but it would not die again. After setting fire to her home with her undead husband inside, Osha ran and did not stop until she escaped south of the Wall, near Winterfell.

There, she was caught trying to steal Bran Stark's horse in the forests surrounding Winterfell, and she was taken back to the castle to serve as penance. Though she has become a devoted caretaker of the Stark children, she, more than anyone else, knows what's arriving along with winter.

After Theon Greyjoy betrays the Starks and captures Winterfell, Osha seduces Theon to help the two Stark boys, Bran and Rickon, escape, along with the powerful but dim-witted Hodor. Osha joins them in their flight, even though she is frightened of the black magic she thinks Bran's visions represent. Ultimately, she refuses to continue with Bran, Jojen, and Meera on their journey north of the Wall. Osha swore she would never return there, and she instead chooses to protect little Rickon on a different path.

GEORGE R. R. MARTIN (CO-EXECUTIVE PRODUCER AND AUTHOR): Natalia, perhaps more than any other person playing a wildling has captured this sense of being half wild. She seems close to nature and only part civilized. In my view, she is mesmerizing to watch.

NINA GOLD (CASTING DIRECTOR): There is only one way to put it really. When you meet Natalia, you realize she really *is* a wild thing.

WARGING:
A BRIEF HISTORY

JOJEN REED: "YOU CAN GET INSIDE HIS HEAD AND SEE THROUGH HIS EYES."

BRAN STARK: "ONLY WHEN I'M ASLEEP."

JOJEN REED: "THAT'S HOW IT BEGINS. UNTIL YOU LEARN HOW TO
CONTROL IT. YOU'RE A WARG."

THOUGH NOT WELL KNOWN SOUTH OF THE WALL, the power to "warg," or to take over the mind of an animal, is an accepted trait among the wildlings. Those with this gift are often used to scout on missions. A warg usually first experiences a transfer during dreams. When his mind is with an animal, the warg's body remains in a vulnerable comatose state. During this experience, should the person's body be killed, their consciousness can remain within the animal and survive. Conversely, if the host animal is killed, the warg will be deeply troubled but will also likely survive.

Warging is not to be confused with the sight—a power to see both the past and the future in vivid dreams, guided by the Three-Eyed Raven.

Bran Stark first experienced warging after he fell from a tower at Winterfell and became paralyzed. Bran, trapped in a crippled body, slowly manifested the ability to meld his mind in dreams with his direwolf, Summer. Bran's joy while running as his direwolf became a temptation he found hard to resist.

Bran's skills, however, continue to grow in startling ways. For instance, after the escape from Winterfell, and after meeting Jojen and Meera Reed, their traveling party is threatened by wildlings. Desperate to protect everyone, Bran successfully enters Hodor's mind and controls him, so that he can use Hodor's physical strength, a terrifying indication of Bran's natural ability.

[OPPOSITE] *Natalia Tena as Osha, the wildling woman.*
[ABOVE] *Bran (Isaac Hempstead-Wright) in the grips of a warging episode.*

— FILMING THE DIREWOLVES —

In season one, the five Stark children—Robb, Sansa, Bran, Arya, and Rickon—plus the bastard Jon Snow, each adopt a direwolf puppy after they find the orphaned litter in the forest near their dead mother. By the end of season three, two of the direwolves are dead, one is lost, and only three are known to be alive. Robb's direwolf, Grey Wind, is killed by Bolton men at the Red Wedding. Sansa's direwolf, Lady, is executed by her father, Ned. This occurs after Arya's direwolf, Nymeria, bites the young prince Joffrey, and Arya drives Nymeria away for her own safety. So, to appease Joffrey, Ned kills Lady in Nymeria's place. Thus, all that remain are Rickon's Shaggydog, Bran's Summer, and Jon Snow's direwolf, Ghost.

STEVE KULLBACK (VFX PRODUCER): At the beginning of season two, we discussed how the wolves would be filmed. By then, we had some experience filming live animals, and that had not been pleasant.

Everyone on the production and at the studio was keen on exploring the possibility of CG wolves. However, when we ultimately sat down with [executive producers and writers] David [Benioff] and Dan [Weiss], we worked through what the direwolves were and what they needed to be—they were essentially just very large wolves. They didn't need to speak languages; they didn't need to perform judo or dance. And the best solution should solve the two most pressing needs: to get the most realistic and threatening possible creature that looks like a wolf and to have it be as least burdensome on production as possible.

We proposed using actual wolves on a green-screen set—taking the animals away from production, and from the actors, as wolves remain dangerous even after training. The reality is, wolves can be trained to do only so much, and that has introduced a challenge in its own right, which the writers sometimes have to work around.

JOE BAUER (VFX SUPERVISOR): The wolves are supposed to be 30 to 40 percent bigger than a standard wolf, so we had "stuffies" built to represent that. These are giant *Game of Thrones*–size dogs, which we carry to the set and shoot for reference and framing, so they leave enough room to accommodate the size of the wolf.

The supervisor will often help the actors create the eye lines, using rigs to indicate the focus or movement. Sometimes it's a stick with a piece of tape on it; sometimes it's a tennis ball on a stick. Then, when we finally shoot the wolves on a green-screen stage, we scale everything down—like the height of the cameras and so on—30 percent from wherever the camera position was when filming the actors. We also shoot at a slightly faster frame rate—say, thirty frames per second rather than twenty-four frames per second—just to slow them down ever so much to accommodate their size, but not so much that they are moving in slow motion. Then we integrate or "marry in" the image of the wolf onto the shot, matching the light of the original day to keep it looking consistent.

[OPPOSITE] *Animal trainers work with the wolves on green screen.*

[ABOVE] *VFX data wranglers position the "stuffie" wolf for a take.*

[FOLLOWING SPREAD] *The CGI direwolf fully integrated into a scene with Jojen Reed.*

"AND NOW HIS WATCH IS ENDED."

— FROM TRADITIONAL NIGHT'S WATCH EULOGY

As they attempt to return to the Wall, the Night's Watch arrives again at Craster's Keep. They are weakened and conflicted, trying to both regroup after their encounter with the undead wights and prepare to meet what is following them. It is sometimes easy to forget the type of men who make up the Watch: hardened criminals, run-aways, and the exiled. Many men have survived, but they are angry, tired, and hungry. At the funeral pyre of one of the men, Craster is blamed for starving them.

Later that night, Craster taunts the strained men and suggests they should just slit their throats and be done with it. Lord Commander Mormont loses control over the mutinous rabble and disaster strikes. Craster is killed by Karl, and Rast stabs Mormont in the back, felling the legendary commander. Brother fights against brother, and the Watch is divided between those loyal to Mormont and those in open rebellion.

ALEX GRAVES (DIRECTOR): On my first night in Belfast, I arrived from L.A. and went straight to the director's dinner. Within about one sentence David Benioff told me that the death of Mormont was probably half the reason they wanted to do the series. Here are these two guys who I want to impress, and I'm thinking, "Now you tell me."

I had all sorts of plans about how I wanted to do it. I wanted it to be at dusk, which is no problem when the days are generally overcast. We get there, and it's the sunniest day they'd ever had at Craster's. Every single shot is hiding sun.

I looked at it like this: Someone is going to die. There's about five minutes before it happens, and there's a musical tempo to it, like a bolero. I was starting to worry about building tension, creating the feeling that something is wrong. It had a lot to do with where Mormont was, where Craster was, and all the guys coming in. You want the audience to ask why they are all there. I got

obsessed with having everyone clocking where everyone else was. I wanted Grenn and Edd to be part of it because they are a big part of this story. I wanted there to be a feeling that something bad was coming and that it went beyond Craster's death.

KIT HARINGTON (JON SNOW): There is something that happens when a young man loses a father, which Jon does: first in Ned and then in Mormont. They take on their role. When Jon finds out that Mormont is dead, this man whom he really did love, he realizes he is sort of out of those father figures. There will be no more. I like to think that Mormont knew he was going to die and was trying to prepare Jon to be ready to pick up that baton.

[OPPOSITE] *Lord Commander Mormont (James Cosmo) leads the battered rangers back to the Wall.* [ABOVE] *The battle begins for control of Craster's Keep.*

GILLY and SAMWELL TARLY

"I DON'T HAVE TIME FOR YOU. I DON'T HAVE TIME FOR ANYONE BUT HIM. BECAUSE HE DOESN'T HAVE MUCH TIME."

—GILLY

Gilly (Hannah Murray) is a young wildling woman and one of Craster's daughters. In fact, Gilly is pregnant with her father's child and terrified about her baby's fate, particularly if it is a boy. While all the children of Craster face dark futures, the boys are under the greatest immediate threat. Soon after they are born, they are taken to the woods and left for the White Walkers.

The first time the Night's Watch, under Mormont's command, arrives at Craster's Keep on their way north,

Gilly appeals to Samwell Tarly (John Bradley) to take her with them when they leave, but Jon Snow will not allow it. When the Watch returns to Craster's, after their defeat, Gilly gives birth to a boy. All she wants is to spend every moment she can with her baby, having lost faith that Sam can help her. However, in the chaos of the mutiny, when Craster and Mormont are killed, Sam takes the opportunity to run away with Gilly and her son, escaping into the forest with the echoes of the carnage following them into the trees.

HANNAH MURRAY (GILLY): When it comes to the escape, she's incredibly animalistic in her need to protect her baby. Her instinct to keep her child alive actually keeps her alive. I'm not sure if she had just chosen to run away and didn't have her son that she would have made it.

For Gilly, every experience or reference relates back to Craster's. It's all she knows, and you can never leave that sort of horror behind. It's such a traumatic and strange world to grow up in. I think about how little she knows.

Gilly is incredibly strong. To take the risk to leave, knowing nothing about the world, is so brave. I think that's part of why she is so important to Sam, too—in this world, she is the lowest of the low, a wildling, a woman, and is still brave. They are very kind to each other, in a way neither has experienced before. I think there is an element for Sam of, if she can be brave, then I can.

JOHN BRADLEY (SAMWELL TARLY): Sam is such an intelligent character, so academic, and is so curious about

knowledge and data, that sometimes he can get wrapped up in those things, in overthinking everything. He is at his best when he forgets it and is instinctive. When he has to find solutions quickly, like with the White Walker, like the escape—that's when he's strongest.

When Gilly tells Sam she's pregnant, he knows what that means—either a horrible violent death or a lifetime of systematic sexual abuse. There is something of a *Schindler's List* moment for him. In Gilly and her baby, he has found someone he can save, something he can fix. He knows what it's like to be damaged by your upbringing, to be scarred by it. In a way, by saving one, by taking a duty of care, he is reclaiming himself from his own childhood.

There is a moment after they have escaped when they are discussing baby names, and Gilly says "Craster." It suddenly strikes Sam that he is the only man she has really known. The only men she would have met would have been Sam, Jon, and Mormont.

None of the other babies would have been given names. Little Sam is the only one to escape. I think it's that moment when Sam decides he wants to prove not all men are like Craster.

HANNAH MURRAY (GILLY): My favorite thing was also one of my first things on *Game of Thrones*—we were rehearsing with [director] Alik Sakharov one of the thimble scenes, and he said to us, "You are two birds with broken wings, and for the first time, when you come together, you realize you might have the possibility of flying." This just broke my heart. It is about two broken people who give each other the strength to be so much more.

[OPPOSITE] *In the chaos of rebellion, Sam and Gilly escape into the forest.*
[ABOVE] *Gilly (Hannah Murray) cradles little Sam.*

— THE WHITE WALKER ATTACKS —
EPISODE 308: "SECOND SONS"

While making their way to Castle Black, Gilly and Sam take refuge in a ruin and build a small fire. Alerted to something outside by the screeching of hundreds of crows, Sam and Gilly *discover that a White Walker (Ross Mullan) has found them and has arrived to take Gilly's child.*

MICHELLE MACLAREN (DIRECTOR): I think what is important in the scene is that Sam's gut instinct takes over and he is a hero. He had to be terrified, but he loves this woman he's trying to protect. John was so great—he really did a terrific job. He's so vulnerable in that moment and you just love him for it.

JOHN BRADLEY (SAMWELL TARLY): Let's not forget that Sam didn't know that he's stabbing the White Walker with a dragonglass dagger. He's working on adrenaline and instinct. He has no sword. He is just thinking, "This is sharp—let's see what this can do." He may be a slayer, but he's lucky.

I was standing on set, and they were doing a shot over my shoulder of Ross, who plays the White Walker in seasons three and four, coming down snaking through these trees. The light was set up perfectly by [director of photography] Chris Seager, and you couldn't see him all the time. You just got flashes of Ross when

he walked past the light, and then he was closer. I was genuinely a little scared; his physical movement is so expressive. He just had this relentless momentum.

HANNAH MURRAY (GILLY): It's so convincing with Ross and all the prosthetics. I remember one of the first takes was John and I running through the woods, with the snow blowing in, and we didn't really know exactly where Ross was. It's always hard to play fear over a period of time—how do you build it up over a scene, to get that tension? It's not ever intellectualized; it's an instinctive place to go. Being in the sets of a show with such high production values helps create that atmosphere.

[ABOVE] *The White Walker (Ross Mullan) reacts to the stabbing.*
[OPPOSITE] *The White Walker destroys Sam's Night's Watch sword.*
[FOLLOWING SPREAD] *Samwell defeats the White Walker with his obsidian blade.*

DRAGONGLASS:
A BRIEF HISTORY

DRAGONGLASS IS THE BEAUTIFUL, DARK VOLCANIC ROCK known as obsidian. It's rare in Westeros and very little is known about it. At the Fist of the First Men north of the Wall, three of the Night's Watch—Grenn, Dolorous Edd, and Samwell Tarly—discover a small cache of weapons buried thousands of years ago but only Sam identifies that the stone weapons are dragonglass. Further, it is only when he is attacked by a White Walker that Sam discovers the true worth of the stone blades. In a moment of desperation, Sam plunges a dragonglass dagger into the creature, the blade begins to smoke, and the White Walker dissolves.

When Sam meets Bran Stark and his traveling companions, Sam shares some of his dragonglass weapons with him. Sam knows that Bran will need them as he ventures north on his own quest.

TOMMY DUNNE (ARMORER): We use real obsidian glass when we can, which is a naturally occurring volcanic glass. It's not something you find everywhere, though there is a good well of it in Mexico. It's quite beautiful but lethal. It has sharpness to it that is unreal. I was very lucky that I had a number of examples from previous jobs that could help us find the look we wanted. The blade has a napped edge; the more you nap it, the sharper it becomes. It's razor sharp when it's done. Access to obsidian is quite restricted because of this.

Taking the piece we want, we start by elongating the style and then sharpening the edges, adding a handle and bindings to it. We can do that all in-house. Once we have a hero blade, which has been shaped and ground into the perfect blade, we can mold it for secondary blades. We'll pour a black silicon rubber, making harder or softer versions, and sometimes fast-cast or plaster, or even hard or soft foam, depending on what the action requires or who will be using it.

Part Two

WARS IN WESTEROS

"With the Tyrells beside us, we'll crush the northerners: hang their lords; burn their strongholds; sow their fields with salt. And no one will think of rebelling for another century."

— Joffrey Baratheon

South of the Wall, the fractured main families of Westeros are too distracted by their ongoing wars to notice the twin threats of the wildling army and the White Walkers. Stannis Baratheon, still reeling from his defeat in the Battle of the Blackwater, remains determined to take the Iron Throne, while Robb Stark continues his own separate, impressive campaign against the ruling House of Lannister. Both are trying to outwit and outmaneuver Tywin Lannister, a master strategist with a single purpose: to consolidate his family's hold on the kingdom and eradicate any threats to the throne. Tywin knows the power to defeat his enemies lies partly in his foresight to make powerful strategic alliances; House Tyrell, with its wealth and power, is preeminent among them.

Meanwhile, Tyrion Lannister, severely wounded in battle and now stripped of his title, continues to negotiate the political dance at court, but now as master of coin rather than as Hand of the King. On the road, Jaime Lannister remains a prisoner of Brienne of Tarth. Arya Stark is still searching for her mother, Catelyn, and Sansa Stark seeks a way out of her hopeless fate in King's Landing, a pawn in a deadly game she is powerless to influence or control.

The wars in Westeros are an unfortunate distraction, for even as the players make their moves, the news from the Wall could change everything.

THE BROTHERHOOD WITHOUT BANNERS:
A BRIEF HISTORY

"THAT'S EXACTLY WHAT WE ARE: GHOSTS, WAITING FOR YOU IN THE DARK. YOU CAN'T SEE US, BUT WE SEE YOU, NO MATTER WHOSE CLOAK YOU WEAR: LANNISTER, STARK, BARATHEON. . . . YOU PREY ON THE WEAK, THE BROTHERHOOD WITHOUT BANNERS WILL HUNT YOU DOWN."

—BERIC DONDARRION

THE BROTHERHOOD WITHOUT BANNERS WAS FORMED after Ned Stark ordered Lord Beric Dondarrion to hunt down and execute "the Mountain," Ser Gregor Clegane. Clegane was seen as a traitor against King Robert Baratheon, and he was wanted for the monstrous crimes he had committed against the people of the Riverlands. Instead, the Mountain killed Beric with a spear through the chest. It was then that the red priest, Thoros of Myr, brought Beric back to life using the powers of the Lord of Light. After his first death, Beric Dondarrion was resurrected multiple times—once after he was executed by the Lannisters after they came to power and declared the Brotherhood the enemy.

Now outlaws, the Brotherhood fights against the injustices being perpetrated against the common folk, predominately by Lannister forces and the Mountain. The Brotherhood is made up of men from all walks of life, including deserters from the Stark and Baratheon armies, farmers, craftsmen, tanners, and masons. They lead small raids and capture men they consider to be the enemy and criminals. Prisoners are either ransomed for funds or put to trial for their crimes in front of the Lord of Light, with Beric Dondarrion acting as his flaming sword.

Tywin Lannister regards the Brotherhood Without Banners as a nuisance, and the Mountain continues to hunt them down, hoping to crush them once and for all.

[PREVIOUS SPREAD] *The power behind the throne: Tywin Lannister advises his grandson, King Joffrey.* [ABOVE] *The Brotherhood relaxes in their forest glade.* [OPPOSITE] *Thoros of Myr played by Paul Kaye.*

THOROS OF MYR

"THERE'S NO STORY SO GOOD A DRINK WON'T MAKE IT BETTER."

—THOROS OF MYR

Thoros of Myr (Paul Kaye) is a priest for the Lord of Light and part of the Brotherhood Without Banners. He was originally sent to Westeros and the court at King's Landing to act as a missionary to Robert Baratheon, hoping to convert Robert to worship the Red God and turn away from the Faith of the Seven.

By his own admission, Thoros of Myr was not a good priest. He chose to sleep with prostitutes and indulge heavily in drinking while in King's Landing. Suffering a crisis of faith, he questioned the existence of all gods. Then, after witnessing the duel in which Beric Dondarrion (Richard Dormer) was slain by Gregor Clegane, Thoros discovered that he had been granted the gift of resurrection.

Thoros still drinks heavily and doesn't wear the robes, but he has renewed faith in the Red God, the one true god in his eyes. Thoros remains fervent in his belief that all men must serve the Lord of Light, a belief that strengthens as Beric is repeatedly restored to life.

ALEX GRAVES (DIRECTOR): I love working with Paul. One of the main things that happened in season three for me was that I fell in love with these two guys [Paul Kaye and Richard Dormer]. I fell in love with their acting. They looked so fantastic; I loved their characters and what they did with them. I loved that when Melisandre comes to the camp, she is both horrified and impressed by Thoros's skills, and that is important. In this world, in the world of the Red Wedding and the executions, the finality of that—Thoros exists.

BRYAN COGMAN (CO-PRODUCER AND WRITER): Thoros was a wonderful surprise for me. For some reason, he didn't register with me as much when I first read the books, but when we started the adaptation process and I was working on my particular episode he ended up being one of my favorite characters to write. We altered him slightly from the book version. In the novel, his partying and drinking days are behind him, having renewed his faith in the Lord of Light. But we thought it would be fun to show both sides of his personality bumping up against each other, so he's still boozing on the show, even after being "born again." I think he's continuing to drink and carouse in order to take the edge off. After all, it's a heavy business bringing someone back from the dead over and over again.

Paul Kaye was extraordinary, one of my favorite additions to the cast in season three. Physically, he wasn't how I pictured Thoros—I'd always imagined him as a corpulent, Friar Tuck type. But Paul brought this kind of grizzled rock star quality to Thoros as well as enormous depth of feeling and focus when it came to the "Lord of Light" scenes. One of the strongest pieces of acting in season three is his monologue to Melisandre, talking about his renewed faith in the Lord of Light.

BERIC DONDARRION

"AYE, I'VE BEEN REBORN IN THE LIGHT OF THE ONE TRUE GOD. AS HAVE WE ALL. AS
WOULD ANY MAN WHO'S SEEN THE THINGS WE'VE SEEN."

—BERIC DONDARRION

Leader of the Brotherhood Without Banners, Beric Dondarrion (Richard Dormer) was killed by Ser Gregor Clegane and then resurrected by Thoros of Myr. Following this experience, Beric Dondarrion converted to the faith of the Lord of Light—as did the rest of the Brotherhood upon witnessing his revival. Beric Dondarrion was subsequently killed and resurrected four additional times. He was stabbed in the stomach, then shot in the back with an arrow, and then had an axe cleave his side. After the Lannisters caught him, they hung him for treason and put a knife through his eye, too.

Then, with Arya and the Brotherhood looking on, Beric duels with "the Hound," Sandor Clegane, and is killed once more. While the Hound's victory proves his innocence in trial by combat, Beric shocks Arya and the Hound when he returns to life. The sixth resurrection is not a full recovery, however, and Beric fears that pieces are being left behind each time. His scars and wounds weigh heavy upon him.

ROBERT STERNE (CASTING DIRECTOR): From the
first time we saw Richard Dormer, we knew we wanted him in
there somewhere. He had the look we wanted. He was what we
wanted.

ALEX GRAVES (DIRECTOR): I never worried about Beric.
Richard gave one of the best auditions I had ever seen. I felt like
we were discovering Alec Guinness. He just was Beric Dondarrion.

RICHARD DORMER (BERIC DONDARRION): I had
actually auditioned several times for the show, for Jaime Lannister,
Jorah, and a few others, but nothing felt right. The first time my
agent gave me the sides for Beric, that changed. There is a slightly
self-destructive element to Beric, the fact that each time he dies
he loses more of himself, but he continues to do what he believes
to be right, tirelessly, endlessly. There is something very dark and
troubled about Beric, but also something kind and noble, and I
loved that he was both.

THE LORD OF LIGHT:
A BRIEF HISTORY

"THE NIGHT IS DARK AND FULL OF TERRORS."

—PRAYER

FOLLOWERS OF R'HLLOR, AS THE LORD OF LIGHT IS KNOWN, have always been few in Westeros, as the religion is predominantly found in the eastern parts of Essos and in the Free Cities.

The Lord of Light goes by many names: the Red God, the God of Flame and Shadow, and the Heart of Fire. Yet the name of R'hllor's enemy is never spoken. Instead, followers speak only of "the Great Other," the god of darkness, cold, and death with whom their god is locked in an endless war.

The faithful believe that one day an unknown person known as "the chosen one" will return with his great sword, Lightbringer, and lend his strength to the Red God's cause.

In the principal temple at Lys, which is considered the largest among all the temples, the red priestess and her priestesses, swathed in crimson robes, pray to the Lord of Light to bring the dawn. Those with great powers are said to see the future among the flames, and some are rumored to be able to resurrect the dead.

[OPPOSITE] *Beric Dondarrion played by Richard Dormer.*
[ABOVE] *Melisandre shows her followers the power of the Lord of Light.*

SANDOR CLEGANE "THE HOUND"

"Kill me, and you're free. But if I live, I'll break both your hands. Go on. Hit me. Hit me hard. You only get one chance."

—The Hound

Sandor Clegane (Rory McCann) is known as the Hound and served as the bodyguard to Joffrey Baratheon until he deserted during the Battle of Blackwater when surrounded by fire. He is known for his great size and the hound's-head helmet he wears in battle. He is the younger brother of the knight known as "the Mountain," Gregor Clegane, one of the most brutal, vicious, and fierce warriors in Westeros. The Hound is badly scarred across the right side of his face, a reminder given by his brother not to play with toys that don't belong to him. While they were only children, Gregor held Sandor down over a roaring brazier, and Sandor most likely would have died if others had not intervened. As a result, the Hound is deeply pyrophobic.

He does not see himself as a knight and will not swear the oath that would make him one, believing that honor is often a shield to hypocrisy. The Hound kills without conscience and is loyal to no one, but he has shown a softness when dealing with Sansa Stark, even offering to take her home to Winterfell in the confusion of Blackwater.

He is captured by the Brotherhood Without Banners and charged with murder. Offered trial by combat by Beric Dondarrion, he must face his greatest fear to fight for his freedom.

[OPPOSITE] *Arya Stark and her unlikely companion, the Hound, after Arya has exacted revenge on a Frey soldier.* [ABOVE] *Beric and the Hound fight to the death, in trial by combat.*

— BUILDING THE CAVE OF FIRE —

At the beginning of season three, production discussed the duel between the Hound and Beric Dondarrion (in Episode 305), which occurs inside a cave. There was little chance of finding a viable cave that was both large enough and safe enough to hold such a fight. They would have to make it, and the challenge was how to build a believable cave indoors. Production designer Gemma Jackson had no doubt it could be done. It's the type of challenge she loves most. For inspiration, she explored the Marble Arch Caves in Northern Ireland, which had already provided the setting for the cave's entrance.

The construction of the cave was a spectacular feat of engineering. To ensure realism, molds were made of the actual Marble Arch Cave walls. First, four coats of silicon were brushed over approximately seven-foot-square areas. The silicon was then covered in plaster and pulled away, leaving behind an immaculate, residue-free, undamaged wall, while creating a perfect copy of every texture, fissure, and cleft in the rock face. These multiple rock patterns and shapes gave the construction team plenty to play with.

Based on the art department design, a clay model was made and cast in plaster. This was marked with a grid that delineated as many as a hundred sections, which were scaled up into "stations" for the full-size cave. Casting plaster the consistency of cream was poured into the rock molds and stiffened with the addition of a jute scrim, then pushed into the mix before timber was added to hold the heavy pieces firm. The rock molds were turned and manipulated to avoid repeating patterns on the cavern walls, and they were fixed together and coated with no less than eight different paint effects to match the Marble Arch rocks. The set painters created the lichen and even the condensation running from the walls.

RORY MCCANN (SANDOR CLEGANE/THE HOUND): The amount of times that I have gotten in trouble for kicking a rock or stone because they seemed real is a compliment to the Art Department and Greens. It looks so authentic inside, with the moss and lichen on the walls. It's not much of a step to believe you are truly in a cave and surrounded by the fires and the Brotherhood, looking old enemies in the eye.

— THE FIGHT —
EPISODE 305: "KISSED BY FIRE"

With any fight sequence, preparation is key. When fire is involved, it is doubly important. Stunt coordinator Paul Herbert and his team were used to working with fire, but safety was paramount. "It can catch you out if you aren't paying attention," he said.

"But fire tends to make people sit up and take notice." The duel between the Hound and Beric Dondarrion involved swinging flaming swords at each other with some force, requiring total trust between the actors.

RORY MCCANN (SANDOR CLEGANE/THE HOUND): Training for this fight required the most training I have ever done. A sword fight with a flaming sword hasn't really been attempted before and we really had to be on our game for that. It took about three weeks, every day to get to where we wanted to be. The fight had to be filmed in sections as the blade would only stay lit for about two minutes. I find that in general the weight of my costume makes a long day exhausting, but the heat of the cave made it even harder to breathe. As soon as take was done, I had to get out and cool down and get air. Richard [Dormer] and I rehearsed, but it all changed when the fire was lit. The sword seemed to grow three feet when the flame appears and it was amazing fighting it. With the sound and the whirling steel with a fire trail, it completely changed the dynamic of the battle. Richard said it was like fighting a crazed King Kong—quite the compliment.

BRYAN COGMAN (CO-PRODUCER AND WRITER): I just assumed the flames would be added later by VFX— I never dreamed the two actors would fight with real fire! Our special effects and stunt teams outdid themselves with that one. And we had both actors going full speed in heavy armor, with a real flaming sword, Rory with makeup on half his face, Richard only using one eye (the other covered with a patch) and they're acting up a storm! It was thrilling to watch—easily one of my favorite sequences in the series.

[OPPOSITE] *Shooting crew and cast share the small cave space and high temperatures.*
[ABOVE] *Thoros uses the power of the Lord of Light to heal Beric.*

— DARKEST MOMENT —
EPISODE 303: "WALK OF PUNISHMENT"

"YOU'RE NOTHING WITHOUT YOUR DADDY. AND YOUR DADDY AIN'T HERE."

—LOCKE

Brienne of Tarth (Gwendoline Christie) has been instructed by Catelyn Stark to escort the prisoner Jaime Lannister (Nikolaj Coster-Waldau) to King's Landing, where it is hoped he is to be exchanged for Catelyn's daughters. However, the journey nearly comes undone when the pair is captured by Locke (Noah Taylor) and his men. Ostensibly Bolton bannermen, they intend on returning Jaime to Roose Bolton and the King in the North. But first the men decide to pull Brienne into the woods to rape her. To save Brienne, and himself, Jaime manages to distract Locke and the others with a lie about the Sapphire Island, which he claims is named for its valuable gemstones. As usual, Jaime expects his charm and status to win the day, making what happens next doubly shocking.

DAVID BENIOFF AND D. B. WEISS (CO-EXECUTIVE PRODUCERS AND WRITERS): We knew this was going to be a moment that really caught people unawares, and more important, a moment that is the beginning of one of the most extreme 180-degree turns we'd ever seen in a character (having read the books). This is where losing a piece of himself puts Jaime Lannister on the unlikely track to sympathy. Which is all a way of saying that we knew we'd better get it right. Luckily for us, the combination of our DP Matt Jensen, AD Mark Taylor, and our amazing stunt team helped us make it everything we'd hoped for and more.

Everyone brought their best to those two nights. Noah had an unusual challenge: he's a very smart guy playing a very smart guy pretending to be a dumb, malleable guy, right until the last minute. He did it so perfectly—watching the scene again, you can really feel the resentment of Jaime's entitlement simmering under the surface from the beginning of their encounter in a way you don't quite catch the first time through. And Gwen is really the catalyst for the scene—it's her jeopardy that causes Jaime to put himself in jeopardy and then step over the line. Her last look to him . . . we love that look. She knows there's something wrong with this set-up, and he's too blinded by his own certainty in himself to get it until it's too late.

And Nikolaj most of all. To play not knowing, not getting it, being too smart by half . . . doing it all that well is impressive enough on its own. Doing it that well when you have a flu that's almost bad enough to shut down the show and send you to the hospital, that's another level entirely. He was graceful and perfect under horrible conditions. Jaime would be proud.

NIKOLAJ COSTER-WALDAU (JAIME LANNISTER): Some actors don't like to know what is coming. For me, it was helpful to know what to aim for. When I was first cast as Jaime, [David Benioff and Dan Weiss] told me the story up through season three. It was so great to know that there was this huge moment coming that would make him question everything about who he is. It meant I could go further in the early seasons.

We were shooting over two days, and as weird as it sounds, I was lucky because I got really sick on the second day. The last thing we were shooting was me being pushed over the stump, and I was really out of it and just felt like vomiting the whole time. There is almost no acting involved. I was being held down, plus Noah is a really scary guy—usually when you are doing a fight on a film, you have to miss by about ten inches, but they had constructed this special arched blade that curved around my arm. Noah just went for it.

Losing his hand was a pivotal moment for Jaime. He really didn't see it coming from Locke. I loved working with Noah. I just thought he was magnificent. I think Locke has something that

I have, which is an issue with entitlement, with people who come from privilege. Jaime refuses to even acknowledge that Locke has the upper hand, and Locke does something rash. It's a huge fuck-you really—he doesn't care about Jaime's father. Jaime has stepped into something he doesn't really understand.

For me as an actor and for Jaime as a person, I think it was the best thing that could possibly happen. I think it forces him to readdress his preconceived notions and rebuild who he is.

GWENDOLINE CHRISTIE (BRIENNE OF TARTH): I think Brienne feels responsible for what happens to Jaime. It's as if he used his one get-out-of-jail-free card to save her and she knows it. I don't think she's ever had anyone save her from anything. It's at this point that she stops protecting him as part of her mission and starts protecting him out of care.

[OPPOSITE] *David Benioff offers Nikolaj Coster-Waldau some direction before the cut.*
[ABOVE] *Locke takes Jaime's greatest weapon.*

JAIME and BRIENNE

JAIME LANNISTER: "MY SWORD HAND. I WAS THAT HAND."

BRIENNE OF TARTH: "YOU HAVE A TASTE, ONE TASTE OF THE REAL WORLD WHERE PEOPLE HAVE IMPORTANT THINGS TAKEN FROM THEM, AND YOU WHINE AND CRY AND QUIT. YOU SOUND LIKE A BLOODY WOMAN."

There is no question that one of the most important relationships in season three is between Jaime and Brienne. They begin as enemies, but when a grudging respect starts to grow, they find themselves questioning everything they once thought about each other. In one of the most revealing scenes of the series (in Episode 305, "Kissed by Fire"), Jaime tells Brienne the true story of how he gained his dishonorable reputation as the "Kingslayer."

In Harrenhal, after the disgraced Maester Qyburn treats the deadly infection on Jaime's severed wrist, Jaime enters the bathhouse. Already in the waters, Brienne is initially horrified that Jaime is determined to share her pool. Further, upon seeing Brienne's look of contempt, Jaime decides to share something even more personal—the origin of his nickname.

As a teenager, when Jaime was in the service of Aerys Targaryen, the country was in revolt. The "Mad King," in his mania, was burning those who displeased him, for he had an obsession with wildfire. When Aerys realized he was losing the war against Robert Baratheon, and a Tywin Lannister-led force was sacking the city, Aerys ordered Jaime to kill his own father, and he told the pyromancer to set the city alight using wildfire he had hidden under King's Landing. To save the city, Jaime killed the pyromancer and the Mad King, slitting Aerys's throat after stabbing him in the back. At this moment, Eddard Stark stormed into the throne room and drew the worst possible conclusion—that the king had been betrayed by one of his sworn protectors.

GWENDOLINE CHRISTIE (BRIENNE OF TARTH): Brienne is this incredible figure, developing this physical strength to overcome the negativity of a male-dominated environment, focusing on her own power—and moreover, to the good of all.

Jaime is the epitome of what she despises, and he tortures and torments her. She has huge contempt for him, no respect at all. He's the Kingslayer, about the least honorable thing you can be, and he seems to show no remorse. Yet he ends up saving her life twice.

ALEX GRAVES (DIRECTOR): They have nothing in common, other than who they are. They are knights, and they understand

something about that. He has protected people he cares about ruthlessly. She is an honorable knight, and he would like to be an honorable knight, but he can't be because he had this awful traumatic thing happen to him.

NIKOLAJ COSTER-WALDAU (JAIME LANNISTER): At the beginning, Jaime has no respect for Brienne. Jaime believes he will kill her eventually. Instead, she reminds him throughout that journey of things that he lost. Really, he's reminded of who he was at sixteen. What he did [when he killed the king] was quite amazing, firstly to be put in a situation like that and then to

still make the right decision, even if it was the most brutal one. Afterward, to be castigated like that—well, that is a real heroic moment. When he tells Brienne the real story, of the potential for genocide, it's probably the first time he has spoken about it.

That's the thing with Brienne; she has earned that trust. He has never met anyone who hasn't tried to better their own circumstances. They kept each other alive. There is a very deep root of respect and understanding. They are both great soldiers. Honor is very important when you have that outlook.

I don't think he's ever shown weakness, but she sees it. When she berates him at the fire, it's because she cares. She's so honest and earnest. He's connected to himself in a way that he cannot undo even when he gets back to King's Landing. He knows what is right and wrong.

BRYAN COGMAN (CO-PRODUCER AND WRITER): It was an incredible gift to be able to adapt that scene, a hugely important scene for Jaime and for the series because it begins the redemption arc of one of the story's central "villains." When season one begins you think you're watching a story about the good Starks versus the evil Lannisters. But it becomes much more complicated than that—in many ways, by season four, the Lannister siblings have become the series' protagonists! (Of course, a lot of that has to do with a lot of the Starks being dead . . .) This scene finds Jaime and Brienne at their most vulnerable, and I think, having carried this burden for so long, Jaime just can't keep it in anymore. He senses a

purity in Brienne and a compassion in her that prompts his confession to just come pouring out of him. He and Gwen and director Alex Graves worked on the scene for a few hours, poring over every line and beat. We shot the scene late into the night—it was very intense and exhausting for all involved. There's the nudity, of course, but also the extreme emotional availability required of the actors and the technical difficulty of shooting in that bathtub for hours and hours. The exhaustion and raw vulnerability you see onscreen are quite real. Nikolaj and Gwen really gave everything they had.

GWENDOLINE CHRISTIE (BRIENNE OF TARTH): I don't think he's been closer to anyone before who never wanted anything from him. I think when humans are confronted by someone like that, it's impossible not to fall in love with them.

She is a selfless character, and in an odd way that runs parallel to Jaime. There is this moment in the bathtub scene when she realizes that he has done this thing—he has sacrificed for the good of thousands of people.

Objectively, I don't think anyone knows the moment that they fall in love. I'm not sure either Jaime or Brienne know themselves well enough for that. She doesn't understand why he rescues her from Locke. After his confession, I'm still not sure she trusts him, but she understands him.

[OPPOSITE] *Enemies fighting on the same side.*
[ABOVE] *Prisoners of Locke, now equals.*

— MARRIAGE OF TYRION AND SANSA —

EPISODE 308: "SECOND SONS"

"WE'RE ALL STRANGERS, AND WE'LL ALWAYS BE STRANGERS, AND THERE IS NO
USE PRETENDING OTHERWISE. BUT I PROMISE YOU ONE THING, MY LADY. I WON'T
EVER HURT YOU."

—TYRION LANNISTER TO SANSA STARK

In King's Landing, Sansa Stark (Sophie Turner) has been cast aside by King Joffrey in favor of Margaery Tyrell, who comes from a rich and powerful house the Lannisters want to be allied with. While a de facto prisoner, Sansa briefly hopes that she might still escape King's Landing when the possibility arises that she will be married to the alluring Loras Tyrell. This is arranged by Lady Olenna Tyrell, grandmother to Loras and Margaery. Lady Olenna is a strategist of the highest order, and she intends to secure the future of her house with another strong alliance. This plan displeases Tywin Lannister, who prefers that Sansa, the potential heir to Winterfell, remain tied to the Lannisters. Tywin swiftly arranges two new marriages—Loras will wed Cersei Lannister, despite Loras's rumored homosexuality, and Tyrion Lannister (Peter Dinklage) is forced to take Sansa as his unwilling bride.

MICHELLE MACLAREN (DIRECTOR): These actors know their characters very well. I like to see what they have prepared and what they want to do. With this scene [of Tyrion and Sansa's wedding], I talked to Peter about the humiliation of this moment, of what Joffrey is doing to Tyrion. With Sophie, it was more about what it means to Sansa when the septon says this is for life. Not too long ago, Sansa thought she was marrying Joffrey and was going to be queen. Then she learns the truth and thinks her escape might be with Loras—she doesn't understand his true desires, but she likes him, and then this happens. Sansa's wedding should be the best day of her life, but in many ways it's the worst. Ironically, though, the person who has been nicest to her is Tyrion. Ultimately, she really grows up in that moment.

Then you have all these other great beats—a look between Olenna and Tywin when you know they have plotted this. Cersei Lannister won't even look at Sansa. She couldn't care less—she's bored by the whole thing and is there only because of her father.

There is a moment in *The Sound of Music* when the camera comes up and over Christopher Plummer and Julie Andrews when they are walking down the aisle. When I was a kid, I wanted a wedding like that, because that's the fairy tale. That's the dream. When I got the script in L.A., I knew I wanted that shot, to shoot it like it was the fantasy when really it's the nightmare. It was so important

to me that it would be like a romantic dream wedding, and for Sansa it should have been—all the elements are there, and it's still just wrong.

PETER DINKLAGE (TYRION LANNISTER): I don't know how hard Tyrion fights the wedding in the end, I think he recognizes that it puts him in a better position to look after Sansa and there is no denying the marriage helps his position in court. It's also true that she has a huge amount of appeal, which he is not immune to, but honor is incredibly important to him in this situation. Tyrion is a man with clear appetites, but he is also in love with Shae. It's an incredibly complex situation.

SOPHIE TURNER (SANSA STARK): It's great to have the relationship between Tyrion and Sansa where (from her point of view) there is a sort of love, but it is based on trust and respect rather than something sexual. He's protecting her from Joffrey, but he also recognizes a strength in her that other people may have missed.

[OPPOSITE] *The unhappy couple.* [ABOVE] *Tyrion cloaking Sansa during their wedding ceremony in the Great Sept of Baelor.*

— COSTUMING SANSA —

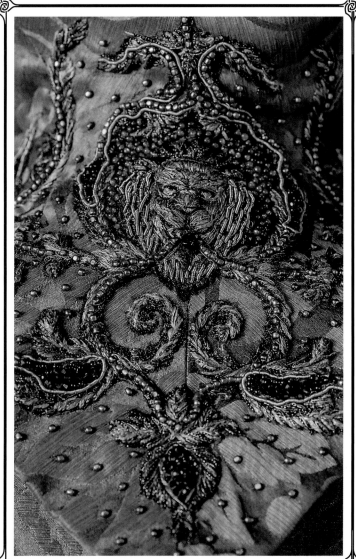

CRAWFORD MCKENZIE (COSTUME CUTTER): We try to reuse as much as possible, so the cape was actually made of the sleeves and skirt from a gown that belonged to Cersei in an earlier season. There was enough to piece them together to form the drape.

Sansa's gown was quite labor-intensive and made with Cersei in mind as a style influence. Handcrafted in imported Italian silks, it took the seamstress Nicki Varney close to two weeks to make, as the fit had to be perfect and was first made up in muslin. The costume armorers hand formed the metal plating on the hips of the dress, first cut and styled in card.

[Costume designer] Michele Clapton then designed the embroidery on the crossover bands, which were then handmade by our embroidery specialist, Michele Carragher.

MICHELE CARRAGHER (EMBROIDER): The straps were created with a more freestyle satin stitch, but I tend to use several colors and metallic threads to create a more 3-D effect. I tend to begin by sketching or painting the plan onto a piece of crêpeline. Then I'll add beads or braiding or little metal rings because, on screen, it can be quite heavy and still not read the detailing.

Michele [Clapton] took her inspiration for the bands from the title sequence of the show, with Sansa's story being told in the imagery. It begins with wolves and fish, and then the wolves are tangling with lions reaching her neck, where a lion head is stamped on the back of her collar.

[OPPOSITE] *Sansa's bridal armor in full.*
[ABOVE] *The lion head and direwolf detail work in the collar of the gown.*
[FOLLOWING SPREAD] *Sansa Stark contemplates her future in King's Landing.*

— BUILDING THE SEPT OF BAELOR —

"I'D LOVE TO SEE THEIR TOMBS, REALLY. IT'S LIKE TAKING A WALK THROUGH HISTORY."

—MARGAERY TYRELL

The Great Sept of Baelor, named for the Septon King Baelor the Blessed, the ninth king of House Targaryen, sits high on Visenya's Hill in King's Landing. As the center of the Faith of the Seven, it holds the tombs of the kings of Westeros. All major religious events that occur in the royal houses of Westeros, like weddings and funerals, take place within its grand interior. The interior of the Sept of Baelor was designed by production designer Gemma Jackson and built for season three in one of the vast cell stages of the Paint Hall in Belfast, next to one of the other key sets for the season, the Wall.

The usable space in Cell 4 of the Paint Hall is a little over 104 feet wide, and the set for the Great Sept took up nearly half of it. It is a massive structure, complete with marble floors with an inlaid seven-pointed star, towering pillars, and handcrafted statues that represent the Seven Gods of the Faith. Of the Sept's fourteen sections, six were built for filming; the remaining walls and ceiling were created and extended by the VFX team in close conjunction with the art department.

GEMMA JACKSON (PRODUCTION DESIGNER): The Sept of Baelor probably represented the greatest challenge for me on *Game of Thrones*. In the end, I found my inspiration in the remains and bones that are said to sit below the Sept. I thought of the burial walls I had seen in the cemeteries of Italy and France, little cabinets placed in stone that hold the urns of ash. I planned the base of the pillars to have little doors and latches, holding within the remains of all that had gone before.

We had huge expectations and extremely limited space, but it was extremely important that we kept the theme of the Seven to represent the Faith. I incorporated the seven-pointed star and the seven pillars, but in doing so I created something of a complication for myself—it's never a straight line of sight from one door to another because the building isn't evenly balanced.

My original design held a good deal more color, but in reality it didn't really sit right. I adjusted the set to a more monochromatic palette, which ended up being an excellent backdrop for the lush colors of the costuming in King's Landing. It also meant

that each section was slightly more anonymous, which allowed each area to be used from a multitude of angles and redressed where necessary.

STEVE KULLBACK (VFX PRODUCER): When we look at the breakdown for any episode, we have to ask, is the scope of what the shot is supposed to be something that could never be realized in construction? Looking at the Sept of Baelor, it needs to be the most extravagant, the most magnificent, the largest, the richest, the most opulent . . . you just can't build St. Patrick's Cathedral on a stage and go and shoot in it. So there is a natural collaboration between the art department and the VFX department to really hone in on what the build will be and what the hand-off to VFX will be.

[ABOVE] *Original art department scale model of the Sept of Baelor set design.*
[OPPOSITE] *VFX exterior of the Sept of Baelor, an interior only set.*

THE FAITH OF THE SEVEN:
A BRIEF HISTORY

IT IS SAID THAT AROUND SIX THOUSAND YEARS AGO, the Seven appeared to the Andals of Essos, who lived in the eastern hills of Andalos. The Seven encouraged them to pursue great conquests, and so the Andals invaded Westeros, bringing their new gods along with their wars.

The Faith of the Seven actually worships a single god who contains seven aspects. Each aspect governs a different part of life. To simplify the concept of aspects, ordained leaders often refer to them as gods in their own right. The highest office or personage is the High Septon, a man who, once in power, discards his common name. Lower orders of the ministry are known as septons, and their female counterparts as septas. The seven aspects or gods are the following:

—THE FATHER—
WHO REPRESENTS JUSTICE AND PRESIDES OVER THE SOULS OF THE DEAD

—THE MOTHER—
WHO REPRESENTS PEACE, MERCY, FERTILITY, AND CHILDBIRTH

—THE WARRIOR—
WHO REPRESENTS COURAGE AND DOMINANCE IN BATTLE

—THE CRONE—
WHO REPRESENTS WISDOM AND IS THE KNOWER OF FATES

—THE SMITH—
WHO REPRESENTS THE CREATOR AND PRESIDES OVER CRAFTSPEOPLE AND FARMERS

—THE MAIDEN—
WHO REPRESENTS INNOCENCE, LOVE, AND BEAUTY

—THE STRANGER—
WHO REPRESENTS THE UNKNOWN AND DEATH

The principles of the Faith decry incest and regicide as two of the worst acts of immorality. The laws of hospitality are seen as the duty of all true followers. Due to the dominance of the religion, these principles have become woven into the laws of the land.

The seven aspects of god lend themselves to many seven-numbered symbols, most particularly the seven-pointed star, which adorns religious buildings and many homes across Westeros. The religion's book of scripture is also known as *The Seven-Pointed Star*. All weddings take place within a star and at the foot of and between the statues of the Mother and the Father.

The Faith of the Seven is the most commonly practiced religion in the Seven Kingdoms. The seat of the Faith is the Great Sept of Baelor in King's Landing. While other faiths and beliefs are practiced, such was the success of the Andals' invasion that to this day the majority of people south of the Neck believe in the Seven.

[OPPOSITE] *The statues of the aspects of the Seven surround the seven-pointed star in the Sept of Baelor.*

PART THREE

THE MOTHER OF DRAGONS

"The Dothraki follow strength above all, khaleesi. You'll have a true khalasar when you prove yourself strong, and not before."

— JORAH MORMONT

ACROSS THE NARROW SEA, DAENERYS TARGARYEN IS GATHERING AN ARMY TO TAKE BACK THE IRON THRONE FROM THE LANNISTERS AND ALL THE WOULD-BE IMPOSTER KINGS OF WESTEROS. HAVING ESCAPED IMPRISONMENT AND WORSE IN THE CITY OF QARTH, DAENERYS SAILS ACROSS SLAVER'S BAY TO ASTAPOR, WHERE SHE PLANS TO PURCHASE AN UNSTOPPABLE ARMY OF THE UNSULLIED. ALTHOUGH DANY FINDS THE IDEA OF SLAVERY REPUGNANT, THIS SLAVE LEGION IS HARD TO RESIST, FOR ITS MEMBERS ARE TRAINED BRUTALLY FROM CHILDHOOD TO BE THE ULTIMATE SOLDIERS.

ASTAPOR IS RULED BY A GUILD OF SLAVERS KNOWN AS THE GOOD MASTERS, WHOSE GOLDEN HARPY SIGIL IS SEEN ALL OVER THE CITY. AS SHE DEALS WITH THE SLAVE MASTER KRAZNYS MO NAKLOZ AND HIS SLAVE MISSANDEI, DAENERYS LEARNS HOW THE UNSULLIED GAINED THEIR MERCILESS REPUTATION AND, FURTHER, WHAT HER OWN LIMITS MIGHT BE.

THE UNSULLIED:
A BRIEF HISTORY

"THEY WILL STAND UNTIL THEY DROP. SUCH IS THEIR OBEDIENCE."

—MISSANDEI

TAKEN FROM THEIR MOTHERS AT THE AGE OF FIVE, THE UNSULLIED are drilled as long as the sun is in the sky each day. They must master all the skills of a short sword, a shield, and three spears. Three of every four boys die during training, leaving the surviving boys with an unquestioning loyalty and no fear of what may happen to them. Made into eunuchs, they are meant to have no desires of their own. They are said to have no life outside their duty; their lives are to be used to fulfill the desires of their masters. Indeed, they are no longer men. To win his shield, each Unsullied must go to the market and kill a newborn child.

When Daenerys lands in Astapor to buy the entire force of eight thousand warriors, they have yet to be tested in battle, nor have they yet killed the required children. She is advised to blood them early . . . which she does, to their former masters' despair.

[PREVIOUS SPREAD] *Daenerys looks over the harbor as her ship sails into Slaver's Bay.* [ABOVE] *The Unsullied lines disappear in the valley.* [OPPOSITE] *The Unsullied forces follow their new queen from the city.*

— COSTUMING DANY —

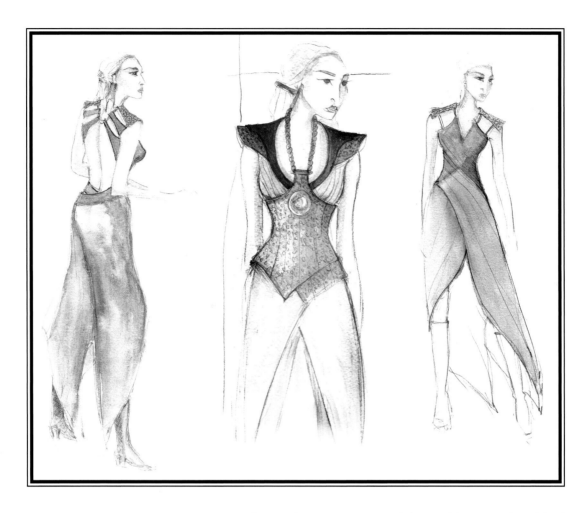

MICHELE CLAPTON (COSTUME DESIGNER): The inspiration for Dany's costumes and their evolution is very much her story. The color choice was dictated by the fact that the Dothraki precious color is blue, so that's really been the basis of her palette. The change in her clothing style is partly about her journey of becoming a woman and a leader, but also the practicality of it. She has been leading a nomadic life and with the riding she has to wear boots and she has to wear leather trousers. The fact that they lend such strength to her look is great, but I wanted the shape to create a sense of her femininity. We looked at so many elements, and we played with dragon scaling embroidery and the sleeves seem almost like the hood on a snake. I wanted to draw in the dragons, but also create a sense of armor, something protective about the choices she makes. After Qarth, where it was designed so that it felt like she had made a mistake in style choice, Dany starts to take on more elements from the male style of dress—because that's where she feels the power is—and then make them her own.

It's a very organic process, so when she gets to Meereen, you start to see similarities between Missandei and Dany. She is still a young woman and she would want to dress like the woman she perceives as her friend, someone who has proved herself as they have traveled together. Dany wants to erase the idea of slave and the separation it causes and that is part of it as well.

EMILIA CLARKE (DAENERYS TARGARYEN): Every season I am completely blown away by not only the beauty and detailing of Dany's costumes, but also the standard. I've been lucky enough to experience couture now and I'm telling you, I look at the costumes and I think—we're better. For me though, my favorite item will always be her boots. It's a love/hate thing: they may be difficult to put on, but they have been everywhere Dany has. They have been filled with blood, they have been filled with snow, they have been filled with sand and mud—they have had it all. They are my favorite bit of Dany. At drama school, it's one of the first things they tell you—if you can't find a character, walk in their shoes—now, those boots, they just make you feel strong.

[ABOVE] *The costume designs for Dany show the running theme of color and shape specific to her character.* [OPPOSITE] *Daenerys takes control and leads her newly acquired Unsullied army.*

EPISODE 304: "AND NOW HIS WATCH IS ENDED"

"A DRAGON IS NOT A SLAVE."

—DAENERYS TARGARYEN

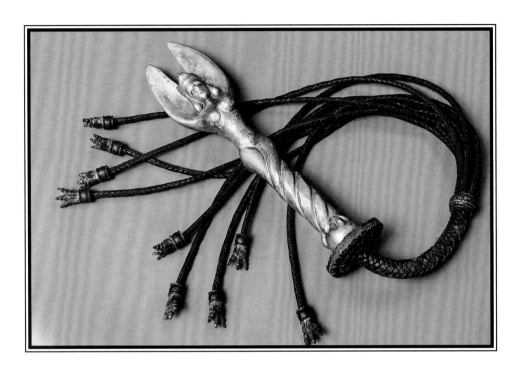

At the end of episode 304, Daenerys (Emilia Clarke) demonstrates her growing strength and determination as a leader. In a spectacular and surprising strategic move, she double-crosses the Astapor slave masters who sell her the Unsullied in exchange for her largest dragon. She simultaneously frees the slaves from their masters, claims her army, and recovers her dragon in a way no one, especially her stunned advisors Jorah Mormont (Iain Glen) and Barristan Selmy (Ian McElhinney), will forget.

ALEX GRAVES (DIRECTOR): Dany's final sequence in the episode was such a massively technical undertaking. It was undoable, unaffordable, and being shot in Morocco on an incredibly tight time scale. I knew from Alan Taylor's season one finale that Emilia was really great. I basically built the whole scene with the idea that she would arrive and then expand every single moment I gave her. I also knew I was going to have fun with Iain [Glen] and Emilia because I had watched the dailies that Dan [Minahan] had shot on the first day, and they were like Hepburn and Tracy.

What I wasn't expecting was for Iain to follow me around for the whole day. I discovered he loves directing and the process. I'd go down to the plaza to talk to Emilia, and I turned round and he was sitting right there. He wanted to know what I was saying that changed her performance. We had a lot of fun. I'm still really proud of that scene because I feel it looks great as the smallest version

of what I could have done if budget was no object. One of the biggest challenges was, how do you film eight thousand guys around one girl when you have only a few hundred extras? I can't even tell you the planning that went into it. I took letter paper representing eight-by-five columns of Unsullied and laid them all over my living room floor with a shot glass as Dany on her horse. I shot them from every possible angle. Then we got to Morocco and some extras didn't show up—so I lost a column and a wide shot. I still think about it.

I set it up so you are seeing her from many different narratives. You see Dany from the Unsullied, you see her standing alone, you see her from the point of view of the masters and Jorah. The audience is left with a feeling of victory, but it's not that straightforward.

There is a subtle moment at the end that I think is important, too—Jorah doesn't fully understand what's going on and warns

Dany against her actions. It's a moment where he realizes he's useless to her now. She's just pulled off the greatest military victory in twenty years and Barristan got it. Jorah didn't and that's not good for him.

DAVID BENIOFF AND D. B. WEISS (CO-EXECUTIVE PRODUCERS AND WRITERS): From the moment we read the scene in the books, we knew this would be a crowd pleaser. The world of the show is so often grim, but this is a place where someone we love triumphs over someone horrible, and does so in a way she completely earns. It's a perfect showcase for her intelligence, her refusal to be backed into false dichotomies, and her ability to find novel (if brutal) solutions to the problems that face her. Emilia was so convincing, by the end of that speech, we really thought she was going to start a revolution.

We were very excited by the possibility of our first real glimpse of the dragons as weapons of war, and director Alex Graves shared our enthusiasm. He even tossed in a freebie shot—which happened to be the plume of dragon-charred guards rising up behind a bad-ass Dany that was one of the key images for the entire third season. The explosion was pretty damn loud, but it was well worth it.

EMILIA CLARKE (DAENERYS TARGARYEN): Season two was quite a frustrating season for Daenerys, because she didn't really get anywhere and her naivety had her coming up against some brick walls. Before we started on season three, David and Dan had talked to me about how there were scenes coming up for Dany that they had been excited about since the very beginning of the whole show so I knew something great was going to be happening. In episode four you get to see Dany take things into her own hands and surprise herself, her advisors, and everyone else around her. The fact it all comes together seems like a sign of things to come. She had started out by asking for advice before making any decisions, although she had proven in season one that she is capable of making bold moves like this by walking into the fire. She's ready to take the risks when that needs to happen. She's also beginning to put the barriers up and beginning to not trust anyone but herself. If she's going to do that, then she really needs to trust in her own instincts.

[OPPOSITE] *The Slaver's whip with the molded harpy handle.* [ABOVE] *Daenerys makes a deal with Kraznys for the Unsullied army.* [FOLLOWING SPREAD] *Daenerys is surrounded as the former slaves call to their new Mhysa.*

CREATING THE ARMIES
OF THE UNSULLIED

Under the heat of the Moroccan sun, with about five hundred extras marching in formation, the VFX department's task was to somehow create the vast Unsullied army in the epic numbers we see on screen.

JOE BAUER (VFX SUPERVISOR): The original intent was to set up the camera at the desired height, which was dictated by the biggest crane available, or 150 feet, and then march everyone through it to capture every possible element.

One advantage of building Astapor in CG was that the main wall was real. Phenomenally, one of the sets from a Ridley Scott movie [*Kingdom of Heaven*] is still standing and formed part of our shooting location. The wall itself is approximately eighty feet high and five hundred feet long. To extend that, we used our crane to take plates of two entirely different locations in Morocco and made them fit together. We shot our shoreline in Essaouira and then the wall in Ouarzazate. In Ouarzazate, we marched the columns of extras, using their movements and positions as starting points to turn the five hundred into eight thousand using replication.

Then the nature of the shot changed quite a bit from what was suggested in the storyboards to what we had the opportunity

to create with effects. That was quite marvelous. Once we opened it up to CG-land, we weren't just panning but could open up the camera and helicopter across. At that point, the march out of the city became an almost entirely CG shot, except for the shoreline.

It's always the goal to be photorealistic, but if you don't have something to look at and match, it's almost impossible to achieve. A photo catches details you might not think of, and if those details aren't there, it doesn't look real—like the backlit dust rising from under the Unsullied's feet, or how the light is hitting the armor inconsistently, or how they walk slightly out of step because, despite their training, they are still human. To be totally in sync would not look right.

[ABOVE] *An Unsullied extra poses for VFX modeling.* [OPPOSITE (TOP)] *The creation of the unit in 3-D.* [OPPOSITE (BOTTOM)] *The Unsullied army before replication.*

THE SECOND SONS:
A BRIEF HISTORY

"MEN WHO FIGHT FOR GOLD HAVE NO HONOR OR LOYALTY. THEY CANNOT BE TRUSTED."

—BARRISTAN SELMY

THE SECOND SONS ARE A MERCENARY FORCE OF APPROXIMATELY TWO THOUSAND MEN who fight for the highest bidder. Their name comes from the fact that a good number of their fighters are "second sons" who will not inherit and must therefore make their own way in the world. The standard of the Second Sons is a broken blade, signifying their ruthless pursuit of victory for their employers and is recognizable across the land.

When Daenerys approaches Yunkai, another slaver city, with her new Unsullied army, she finds Yunkai is protected by the mercenary Second Sons, who are led by three men: Mero, Prendahl na Ghezn, and Daario Naharis. Dany offers an alliance with the Second Sons if they will break their contract with the Yunkai, and she gives them two days in which to decide. Although the captains plan to assassinate Daenerys, Daario Naharis silently decides he prefers to fight for beauty—and so he brings the other captains' heads and the Second Sons numbers to her.

[ABOVE] *Daenerys plans her campaign with her military advisors.*
[OPPOSITE] *The Second Sons' camp below the Yunkai city walls.*

PART FOUR

THE RED WEDDING

"Roslin caught a fine fat trout. Her brothers gave her a pair of wolf pelts for her wedding."

— WALDER FREY TO TYWIN LANNISTER

As the wars between the factions of Westeros continue apace, strategy and strength in numbers remain two of the greatest factors in the chances for success. After beheading Lord Karstark for insubordination, Robb Stark has lost his bannermen, weakening his numbers. Determined to press his advantage while his victories are still fresh, Robb plans to bring his forces to the Lannister's door at Casterly Rock—an audacious move that, if successful, could end the conflict for the Starks and see Robb as King. To do this he needs one thing, the forces belonging to Walder Frey, Lord of the Twins, whom he snubbed when he reneged on the deal brokered by Catelyn Stark when the campaign began.

HOUSE TULLY:
A BRIEF HISTORY

"IT OFTEN COMFORTS ME TO THINK THAT EVEN DURING WAR'S DARKEST DAYS, IN MOST PLACES IN THE WORLD, ABSOLUTELY NOTHING IS HAPPENING."

—SER BRYNDEN "BLACKFISH" TULLY

WITH A NOBLE HISTORY STRETCHING BACK TO THE AGE OF HEROES, House Tully has held the seat of Riverrun at the fork of the Trident in the Riverlands for more than a thousand years. The Tullys have never held the title of king, but since the Wars of Conquest each lord of the house has been known as Lord Paramount of the Trident.

During his reign, the much-despised tyrant Harren the Black of House Hoare ruled over Riverrun. When Aegon the Conqueror swept north with his dragons, Lord Edmyn Tully was the first to join his forces and rebel against Harren. After Aegon's victory, Lord Edmyn was granted the title of Lord Paramount, with all the other lords of the region owing him fealty.

The Tullys have always made strong alliances through marriage. At the age of twelve, Catelyn Tully, the eldest child of Hoster Tully, was promised in marriage to Brandon Stark to strengthen the ties to Winterfell, from where the Starks governed the North.

However, Brandon Stark and his father were killed by the "Mad King" Aerys Targaryen, which sparked the war known as Robert's Rebellion. To maintain the ties between the great houses, Catelyn was married instead to Brandon's younger brother, Eddard Stark. Meanwhile, Catelyn's sister, Lysa, was wedded to Jon Arryn, Lord of the Vale.

More recently, after the murder of Jon Arryn and the execution of Eddard Stark, as well as the ascendance of the Lannisters to the throne, House Tully finds its alliances strained and in flux. They have pledged to support Robb Stark, Catelyn's son, who has been dubbed the new "King in the North," thus sacrificing any connection to the Lannisters' court.

[PREVIOUS SPREAD] *A king in love and his loving queen.* [ABOVE] *Robb stands with his mother, wife, and uncle at the funeral of his grandfather.* [OPPOSITE] *House Tully family tree.*

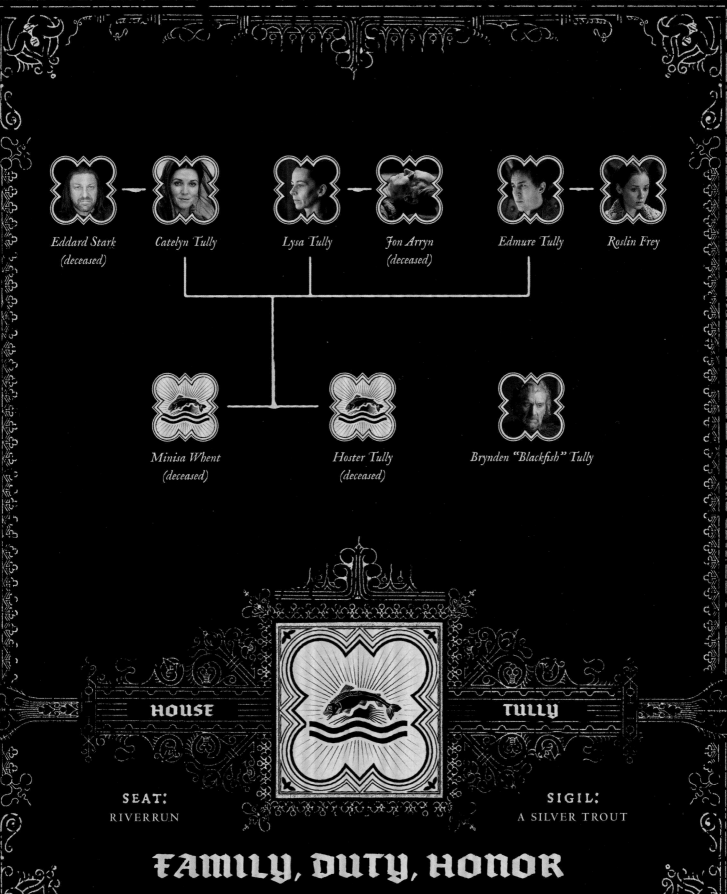

Eddard Stark
(deceased)

Catelyn Tully

Lysa Tully

Jon Arryn
(deceased)

Edmure Tully

Roslin Frey

Minisa Whent
(deceased)

Hoster Tully
(deceased)

Brynden "Blackfish" Tully

HOUSE · TULLY

SEAT:
RIVERRUN

SIGIL:
A SILVER TROUT

FAMILY, DUTY, HONOR

BRYNDEN TULLY
"BLACKFISH"

"PEOPLE HAVE BEEN CALLING ME 'BLACKFISH' FOR SO LONG, THEY DON'T KNOW MY REAL NAME."

—SER BRYNDEN TULLY

Brynden Tully (Clive Russell), better known as Blackfish, is the younger brother of Hoster Tully and uncle to Catelyn, Edmure, and Lysa. Known as an excellent commander and strategist, he has little patience for the ineptitude of his nephew, Edmure, but despite his frustration, his love is steadfast and he honors his family above all else.

After Lord Hoster dies, Blackfish acts as a military advisor to Robb Stark. Most significantly, he brings Lord Rickard Karstark before Robb for the murder of two Lannister prisoners whom Robb had pledged to protect, despite direct orders that they were to remain unharmed.

Robb is urged to reconsider his sentence of death, but ignores the advice and beheads Karstark, and in doing so, he loses the allegiance of Karstark's bannermen, who make up half of the forces of the North.

Later, to help Robb Stark repair his alliance with House Frey, Blackfish is instrumental in pressuring Edmure to marry Roslin Frey in Robb's place. Blackfish steadfastly reminds Edmure of his previous mistakes and need to support his king. Unaware that this alliance will be betrayed at the Red Wedding, Blackfish leaves before the massacre begins. His current whereabouts remain unknown.

MICHELLE FAIRLEY (CATELYN STARK): Clive Russell is just the most incredibly wonderful, caring, and shy guy, but also a spectacularly experienced actor. I had the advantage of working with Clive before, so welcoming him to such an established show became very easy. I think it also helped with the relationship Catelyn has with her family, which I believe is quite troubled. There's a good deal of acceptance from Cat that her family members are the way they are and they should just get on with it, but an uneasy history, too. I loved my scenes with Clive, particularly when they are discussing Hoster's death. He's the sort of actor you trust implicitly, to talk when you need to talk or wait when you need to wait. He's a very wise and honest man.

EDMURE TULLY

EDMURE TULLY: "HE'S GETTING ME. A TULLY OF THE TRIDENT, LORD OF RIVERRUN."

BRYNDEN TULLY: "HERO OF THE STONE MILL."

Edmure Tully (Tobias Menzies), the youngest son and heir of Hoster Tully and now Lord of Riverrun, remains something of an irritation to his uncle Blackfish. Edmure has been fighting for Robb Stark, his nephew and also his king, but he is arrogant and foolish and lacks strategic skill. After an important battle in which he impulsively gives up a key strategic position for a minor victory and low-grade Lannister prisoners, Edmure is compelled to make amends to Robb for this miscalculation by marrying Roslin Frey in his king's place. Edmure resents this, but he capitulates under strong pressure from his family.

When the Stark and Tully forces arrive at the Twins for Edmure's wedding, Walder Frey makes a great show of reconciliation. Until now, Edmure has not seen his bride, and Frey's unattractive brood makes his sacrifice seem all the more daunting. However, when Roslin is revealed, Edmure is delighted with her beauty. After much celebration, and following custom, Edmure and his bride are eventually whisked from the main room for the ceremonial bedding. But once the doors are bolted, locking them inside, the carefully planned massacre of Robb Stark and his bannermen begins. All information suggests that Edmure, Lord of Riverrun, spends his wedding night in a cell, at the Twins, and that he is likely to remain a prisoner for some time to come.

MICHELLE FAIRLEY (CATELYN STARK): I loved the writing for Edmure. I adored the way that David [Benioff] and Dan [Weiss] wrote him to be so arrogant, petulant, and stupid. At the same time, I think if you are a forward-thinking person, you know not to attack someone like that. You try and give them room to grow. Instead of the black sheep, he is the weak sheep. It's an easier dynamic between Robb and Blackfish. They understand each other, have a similar mind-set. For Edmure, I think most of the acceptance is coming from Catelyn, who just wants to encourage him to be better than he is.

[OPPOSITE] *Blackfish in costume, each doublet made of 1000 hand-cut and sewn leather scales.* [ABOVE] *Edmure Tully takes aim for the second time.*

HOUSE FREY:
A BRIEF HISTORY

"LET'S GET READY. THE WINE WILL FLOW RED, AND THE MUSIC WILL PLAY LOUD, AND WE'LL PUT THIS MESS BEHIND US."

—WALDER FREY

IN THE RIVERLANDS, STRADDLING THE TRIDENT AT THE GREEN FORK, is the dual tower castle known as the Twins. Its two tall, gray towers embrace over the crossing—and form the only available river bridge for hundreds of miles in either direction. The strategic position of this fortress has allowed the Frey family to grow wealthy and strong from the tolls they have collected from travelers for more than six hundred years. The current Lord of the Crossing is Walder Frey, an old man now married to his eighth wife and father to more children than he can count. Walder Frey knows that control of this confluence is a priceless military asset to anyone with designs on the Iron Throne. Initially, he agrees to form an alliance with Robb Stark, the King in the North, after Catelyn promises that Robb will marry Frey's daughter Roslin.

When Robb betrays this promise and marries Talisa Maegyr instead, Walder is beside himself with rage and humiliation at the perceived slight. He withholds his forces from Robb's campaign. Later, when Edmure Tully is offered as a replacement husband for Roslin, Walder is apparently mollified; he agrees to the marriage and to repairing the alliance. Walder even invites the Stark forces to the Twins for the union, offering them a brief respite from their constant battles and a chance to renew their strength in numbers against the Lannister armies.

In fact, the wedding is a trap, planned by Walder Frey to punish the Starks and the Tullys and to change the balance of power in Westeros forever.

[ABOVE] *Walder Frey has a villainous plan, but a beautiful child.*
[OPPOSITE] *House Frey family tree.* [FOLLOWING SPREAD] *The banquet hall at the Twins, as Walder Frey plays host to the Red Wedding.*

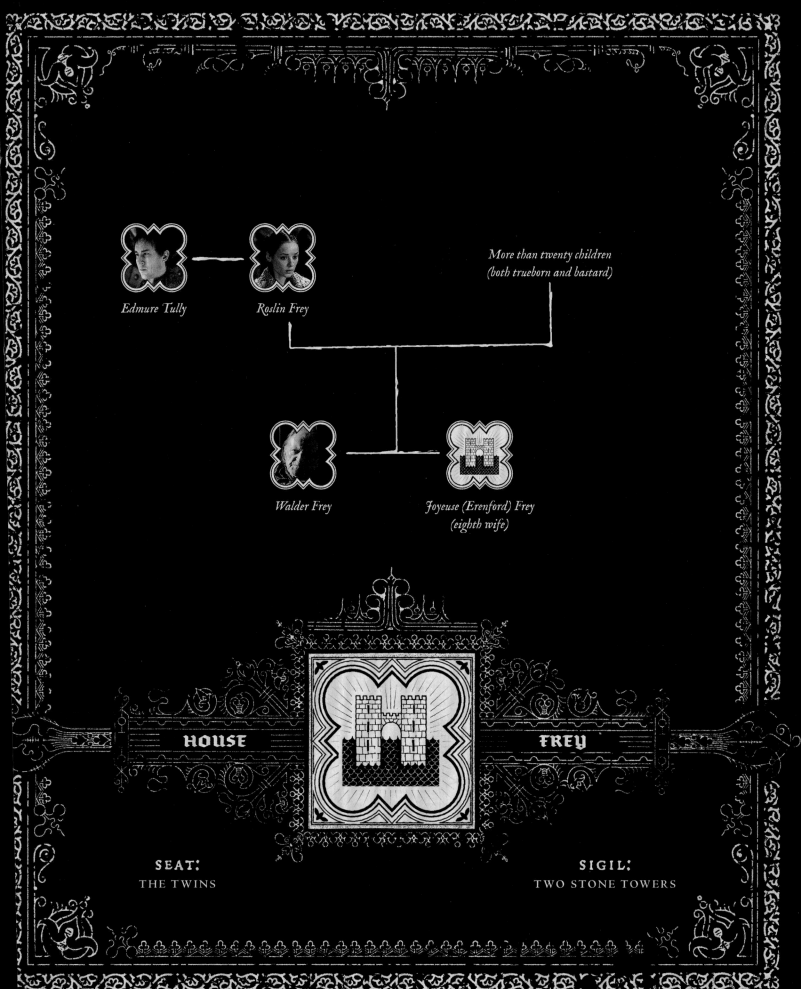

Edmure Tully — Roslin Frey

More than twenty children
(both trueborn and bastard)

Walder Frey

Joyeuse (Erenford) Frey
(eighth wife)

HOUSE   FREY

SEAT:
THE TWINS

SIGIL:
TWO STONE TOWERS

— THE RED WEDDING —
EPISODE 309: "THE RAINS OF CASTAMERE"

"I HAVEN'T SHOWN YOU THE HOSPITALITY YOU DESERVE. MY KING IS MARRIED
AND I OWE MY NEW QUEEN A WEDDING GIFT."

—WALDER FREY

The "Red Wedding" begins as a rare moment of happiness that, ultimately, becomes one of the most devastating sequences in the show's history. Initially, the wedding of Edmure and Roslin is filled with much hope. Edmure is overjoyed to discover that Roslin is a woman of remarkable beauty, and the strained relationship between Walder Frey and the Starks seems to ease. For the Stark family, it's a chance to imagine a more peaceful future. Robb and Talisa discuss raising their unborn child, and Catelyn is relieved by the renewal of the Frey alliance. The bride and groom leave the hall to complete the bedding ceremony in a raucous parade of well-wishers. After discussing the quirks of family, Blackfish Tully excuses himself to find another kind of relief after too many flagons of ale.

Then, ominously, the doors are closed. Catelyn notices that Roose Bolton is wearing armor hidden under his clothing, a clear indication that the wedding is not what it seems. Walder

Frey speaks, offering his king the hospitality he deserves and his queen a gift, and with these mocking double entendres, the carnage begins. Catelyn screams a warning as Talisa is brutally stabbed in the stomach, killing both her and the baby in her womb. As Robb tries to reach her fallen body, crossbow bolts rain down, and the haunting chords of "The Rains of Castamere" play among the echoes of fighting and murder.

Catelyn seizes Walder's young wife, Joyeuse, and asks for Robb, now struggling to stand, to be granted mercy. Walder mockingly refuses, and Roose Bolton, saying "the Lannisters send their regards," drives a dagger into Robb's heart. Catelyn can only watch in helpless agony. Then, in retribution, she kills Joyeuse, slitting her throat. As the last to fall, Catelyn bears witness to the horror of seeing her worst fears realized—until her own throat is opened by Black Walder, one of Frey's great-grandchildren, and she slips into darkness.

DAVID NUTTER (DIRECTOR): Toward the end of season two, David [Benioff] and Dan [Weiss] started to whisper in my ear about being involved with the Red Wedding. I had deliberately not read the books. I wanted to be led by the scripts when it came to storytelling, and I didn't want to get ahead of myself. Once I had agreed to be involved, I started to read about it, to get a sense of the sequence. Then, this weight appeared above my head, and I had all this trepidation and nervousness for about nine months before we even started on it. My initial feeling was simply fear. When the scripts arrived, that's when it became about breaking down how it was going to work.

Meeting Walder Frey initially, that scene was pretty clear-cut for me, as was the wedding—but the feast, well, that was more complicated. It was important for me, like a coach at a football game, to figure out what all the plays were going to be and how best to manipulate that. Where the characters were going to be and the interactions: Robb and Talisa and Catelyn watching them, where was Walder and Lothar Frey, and the importance of Roose

Bolton. I sat down with [production designer] Gemma Jackson to discuss the sets, how the tables should be. That, to me, once I could get that figured out, was one of the biggest challenges. It was written so very well. It had to be joyous and raucous, but there also had to be a sense of ease—finally something nice is going to happen. It was so important to have that lull, with Robb and Talisa talking about their baby and Catelyn starting to see that and thinking they are going to be all right before the tables are turned.

It was very important to me that it was shot in sequence. I come from a musical background, and in a way this is like a piece of music. It was key that we had very little wasted time. I wanted to shoot it in sequence so the actors could give it their all, that there would be no holding back in those final moments.

[OPPOSITE] *A king stands betrayed.*
[ABOVE] *A moment of peace for the Stark family.*

GEORGE R. R. MARTIN (CO-EXECUTIVE PRO-DUCER AND AUTHOR): I knew years before I got to the scene that Robb was going to die. From the beginning he was marked for death. People have said that he should have been a POV character and in retrospect maybe he should have been, because then it would have been even more of a shock, but I always knew he was going to die. I wanted to deconstruct the usual fantasy thing and I had already killed Ned. In 90 percent of fantasies the father is murdered and the son picks up his mantle and avenges him. I wanted a switch, where you seem to be getting the heroic son, but whoops—he's dead, too. While writing, I made some other decisions about that scene. Catelyn was going to have to die and the army needed to be destroyed, too. It's very loosely based on two incidents in Scottish history. One was the Black Dinner, where Black Douglas was promised safe passage to the royal place at Stirling to meet with the King and settle their differences, but at the dinner both he and his brother were murdered. The other is, of course, the famous massacre of Glencoe where the guests who were protected by guest-right killed their McDonald hosts in the middle of the night. I used that as a basis, but added my own fantasy elements.

MICHELLE FAIRLEY (CATELYN STARK): [Filming the scenes] in chronological order was incredibly difficult because there was an emotional crescendo. But, honestly? It was one of the best weeks of my working life. You are surrounded by completely wonderful craftspeople, the crew, who after three years are your

friends. It's a time for saying good-bye, but you keep in mind what you are here to do. It's the best thing in the world to be trusted with material like that, to be able to do it. It was exhausting on the final wrap. It was a palpable thing—there was a surge of energy at the end. I think we all felt it.

DAVID BENIOFF AND D. B. WEISS (CO-EXECUTIVE PRODUCERS AND WRITERS): David [Nutter] came into this knowing full well how powerful the scene could be if done right. He prepared accordingly. He is a Terminator—a man who can shoot the hell out of a battle in two days and wrap early. He showed up at the first story meeting with reams of charts and diagrams—he had the whole thing staged in his head from the get-go. This degree of organization gave him the efficiency needed to do full justice to every single moment. And there are many, many little moments.

David worked so well with the actors, who all brought everything they had to this one. Everyone: Oona, Michael, David, Maisie, Rory . . . and Richard and Michelle. It almost seems redundant to talk about the strength and perfection of their performances in this scene. There was something very emotionally honest in their sadness, and in everyone's sadness at seeing them go. [They were surrounded by a tough, Northern Irish crew who were tearing up at the monitors. The makeup department needed their own makeup department.] From the pilot, Richard and Michelle have been lodged at the beating heart of the show, so beautifully and powerfully embodying the complex and ultimately

loving relationship between mother and son. The idea that they're not still on the show hasn't sunk in yet, and probably never will.

GEORGE R. R. MARTIN (CO-EXECUTIVE PRODUCER AND AUTHOR): I didn't see the rough edit. I had hoped to come to set for the Red Wedding and be a Stark casualty, having my throat cut in the background, but sadly the press of work did not allow it. When I did see the final cut it was so vividly and viscerally done, I really felt that David and Dan had turned it up to an 11 in some senses. I knew we would get a huge reaction, because I had gotten a huge reaction 13 years ago—I got the emails and letters from people, some saying I was brilliant, some saying they would never read another book, some hoping I would die in a fire. With TV being much bigger and the Internet being prevalent, I knew it would be big, but I didn't realize just how big. It's pretty visceral in the books and to be honest I didn't think that anyone would be able to make it bloodier, but David and Dan brought in Talisa and then made her pregnant. That had an impact even on me, because I wasn't sure if she would end up at the wedding.

MICHELLE FAIRLEY (CATELYN STARK): I've watched it only once. I find it very hard. The speed of it, the way it was cut and edited, you felt you were there. Where would you run if you were in there? Even before Catelyn realizes what's happening, there is this relentless inevitability to it. I think, in many ways, she was

hoping, going against her gut that everything was going to be okay, but the minute the music starts it confirms her fears.

DAVID NUTTER (DIRECTOR): Michelle Fairley is basically one of the greatest actresses. Seriously—she lives Catelyn Stark. There is nothing for me to do. There is a sequence when Black Walder has locked the doors and the music is playing—she knows something is very, very wrong. We played a recording of the music and had the band there so she could react to it. Once she realizes Roose Bolton is in on it, she disregards herself completely. She is a mother trying to protect her son. You can see her lose her will to live before she dies herself. Her performance was magnificent.

RICHARD MADDEN (ROBB STARK): I deliberately didn't read any books ahead of each season; I didn't want to know or preempt myself. I liked that each step took him closer to reaching his potential, but I needed it to be a surprise for me.

That said, I was aware of the Red Wedding from the beginning. David and Dan explained just how big the sequence was and how in many ways, the series was about getting to that place. After that, lots of people were more than happy to fill me in before I got to it in the books.

[OPPOSITE] *The royal couple, before the tragedy.* [ABOVE] *The Great Hall at the Twins with a dolly track to catch the murder of the bannermen.*

It was hard to film, but what I tried to do was to block it out while filming during that week. I was keen not to anticipate anything in my actions. I wanted it to be clean, because Robb doesn't know what is going to happen. I wanted to be able to play those scenes with honest joy and relief, because that is what Robb would have been feeling. In the end, it felt like a surprise to me, because Robb didn't see it coming. Really, it's only Catelyn who does.

Working with Michelle [Fairley] was amazing. In every new job as an actor you are put in a situation where you have to throw yourself into it and just trust another actor. We ended up with a friendship that allowed us to start a scene in a place you never could with a person you had only just met. We already have the layers, the history of what we have already been through to build on. Michelle is an actress who you look in the eye and it's very hard not to tell the truth with because she is so honest in her performance.

Robb and Catelyn have been on such a relentless journey. In many ways, Robb is like his father, which is also partly why their dynamic is so strong. It's also something that drives the devastation— of all the marriages we have seen in Westeros, only Ned and Catelyn and Robb and Talisa are marriages of love. That's part of the injustice of the situation. It's born of something good. Yes, he broke his oath and his vows, but it's like he was too young for it. I think he ended up there because of what was going on around him, with all the loss and betrayals to then have someone honest and loyal—well, maybe there was a world where things could have worked differently. In the end what we do have is a really great love story between the two characters. I think that's what makes it harder on Catelyn—she can see that it's honest and pure and she

knows he's doing the right thing to follow his heart, even if it's the wrong thing politically.

That's where the Starks fall down really; they follow their hearts and do what is fair and honest and just and not simply the right political move.

I didn't go into the scene with any expectations of reaction. All I wanted was for it to be as surprising as it was in the books. I had it in my head that I wanted it to show him never giving up, even when the arrows are in him and Roose comes at him with the knife, that he would just keep fighting until his body stopped working. Then, when I got to that point I realized something about Robb. It wasn't just about fighting until you can't go anymore. There was a change in him, when Talisa went and he knew it was over. There was almost a relief to it. When he says "mother," it's as if he is saying "we can be at peace now." They had been in such turmoil, fighting, fighting and never stopping trying to get everyone back. In hindsight I look at Catelyn and Robb and they were only ever fighting to keep each other alive.

It changed for me on set. He didn't want to fight anymore. What are they fighting for, vengeance? He believes his family is dead. He's won all these battles and done so well at being a man and this leader. Then he resigns when he's lost the fight, and it gives him calm.

[ABOVE] *The camera gets the perfect angle.* [OPPOSITE] *The pure anguish of Catelyn Stark.* [FOLLOWING SPREAD] *After the mayhem of the Red Wedding, the Hound begins a new stage of his journey, now as Arya's protector.*

SEASO

N IV

Part Five

RESETTING THE GAME

"Our alliance with the Lannisters remains every bit as necessary for them as it is unpleasant. The Iron Throne may be the worst chair in the world, but they're not through sitting in it."

— LADY OLENNA TYRELL

AFTER THE RED WEDDING, THE MAIN THREAT TO THE LANNISTERS' HOLD ON THE IRON THRONE HAS BEEN ELIMINATED. ROBB STARK IS DEAD, HIS FORCES HAVE BEEN MASSACRED, AND HIS ALLIANCES ARE IN TATTERS. YET PEACE AND SECURITY REMAIN ELUSIVE AT KING'S LANDING. STANNIS BARATHEON STILL PURSUES HIS CLAIM TO THE THRONE, AND ACROSS THE NARROW SEA, DAENERYS TARGARYEN IS NURTURING DRAGONS AND GATHERING AN ARMY IN PREPARATION FOR HER OWN ARRIVAL IN WESTEROS. MEANWHILE, UNSETTLING NEWS FROM THE NORTH INDICATES TWIN DANGERS: AN ADVANCING WILDLING ARMY FOLLOWED, SO RUMOR HAS IT, BY THE LEGENDARY UNDEAD WHITE WALKERS.

FURTHER, EVEN THE LANNISTERS' MOST IMPORTANT ALLIANCE, WITH HOUSE TYRELL, REMAINS FRAUGHT WITH POLITICAL GAMESMANSHIP, AND NEW PLAYERS, SUCH AS HOUSE MARTELL IN DORNE, ARE STEPPING OUT FROM THE SHADOWS, EAGER TO MAKE THEIR OWN MOVES.

BUILDING THE FORGE,
— CASTING THE SWORDS —

The opening episode of season four (Episode 401, "Two Swords") includes a scene that is only a few minutes long. There is no dialogue. There is no violence. Instead, we simply watch as Ned Stark's iconic blade Ice is melted down to create two new swords for Jaime Lannister and King Joffrey. This represents something that by now all viewers know—the Lannisters have subdued and, for the moment, vanquished the Starks.

The scene's brevity belies the immense work that went into filming it. Over several months, a working forge was built into the cellars of one of the buildings of Shane's Castle, just outside Belfast, and numerous technical tests were run by the SFX department. Offsite, prop elements representing every stage of the smithing process were ready to be used: billets (unfinished blades) swapped in or out to be worked on depending on the requirements on a shot, some pre-forged with fullers (grooves along the length) and some ready to have them added. The stage was set.

The first day of filming was an unusually hot day in July, and the temperatures inside the confined set were over 100 degrees Fahrenheit (38 degrees Celsius). As the heat rose to the arched ceilings, hundreds of tiny spiders threaded down into the room, dangling only a few inches above the heads of the crew, while the blacksmith (armorer Tommy Dunne) and his assistant (assistant armorer Steven Murphy) worked on the blades.

TOMMY DUNNE (ARMORER): Playing the blacksmith was a bit of an in-house joke, which I wasn't sure was going to really happen, but it was great to be involved on screen. Both Steve and I had a great time on the day. During filming, we couldn't really work as we would in reality. We had plenty of premade swords: one billet of full fatness, semi-beaten, half beaten, half drawn, quarter drawn (which is essentially a thinner blade), no fullers, partial fullers, and completed fullers, which could be swapped into a shot as needed. The original Ice blade is quite safe. SFX created a wax melt and aluminium bronze alloy to "cheat" the process.

STUART BRISDON (SFX SUPERVISOR): We wanted to get the fantastic look of the real metal pour, so we made our own smelter and melted down bronze in a ceramic crucible. A lot of the work was done by Laurence Harvey, one of our senior SFX technicians. We chose to use bronze for this element of the shoot, even though it was the wrong metal, because it had the lowest melting point and that made it easier to work with. The crucible that held the molten alloy could withstand heats of up to 1,200 degrees Celsius [2,190 degrees Fahrenheit], and when full it weighed around twelve pounds. To add to the visual impact, we added charcoal dust to the areas the metal would run, causing tiny flares as it ignited. We fixed a cinnamon shaker on a long pole above the forge, which sprinkled coal dust over the pour and forge to create sparks for the camera.

Originally, we had hoped to do the melt of the blade for real, but in the end we found that it was simply too impractical. So we started working with wax that could be melted quickly and

efficiently. During the testing process, we discovered that if you added fluorescent orange dye to the wax and then lit it from beneath with an ultraviolet light, it took on the appearance of molten metal. The only downside was that this could not be done on the actual forge, so for the actual melt, we had to build a special heatproof glass mold insert with heated elements and the light underneath creating the glow.

Laurence was also responsible for building the forge. In a real forge, the hot area is actually a very limited space, but we wanted a larger flamed area. The forge got up to such temperatures underneath that a cooling system was constantly running to cool the gas pipes and run through the jackets that surrounded the burners so they didn't melt in the heat. The tank reservoir outside was actually boiling at some points during the day.

TOMMY DUNNE (ARMORER): The final blades for Joffrey and Jaime were my designs. I like to design things in my head, knowing the Lannisters and the need for them to be both ornate and highly luxurious. Incorporating the lion's head in a way that hadn't been seen before was a bit tricky. Previously, it's been an impression—this year I wanted to create something that included the whole head and had the cross-guard coming out of a pommel textured with the lion's fur. I was very fortunate to work with the concept artist Peter McKinstry, who realized my design by looking at the elements in the workshop and an in-depth description.

[PREVIOUS SPREAD] *Joffrey and Margaery are bound together in marriage.* [OPPOSITE] *Concept painting of the completed forge.* [ABOVE] *The VFX team oversees the pour of molten bronze for the close-up shot.*

HOUSE TYRELL:
A BRIEF HISTORY

"Roses are boring, dear. 'Growing Strong.' Ha! The dullest words of any house."

—Lady Olenna Tyrell

RULING OVER THE RICH AND FERTILE LANDS OF THE REACH from its seat in Highgarden, House Tyrell is the foremost noble family in Westeros, with their wealth and military strength second only to the Lannisters. Historically, the Tyrells were stewards to the kings of the Reach, but this changed when the last king, Mern IX, was killed by Aegon the Conqueror during the blood-soaked battle at the Field of Fire. After Aegon's victory, it was the duty of the steward, Lord Harlen Tyrell, to surrender for his fallen king. When Tyrell pledged fealty to the new Targaryen ruler, Aegon granted the Tyrells dominion over the Reach and named them Wardens of the South, lending the family all the power and wealth of the position.

Later, when Robert Baratheon and Ned Stark rebelled against the Mad King Aerys, the Tyrells remained steadfastly loyal to the Targaryen royal family. However, their loyalty didn't outweigh their pragmatism. After Lannister forces claimed victory at the Sack of King's Landing, and the Targaryen dynasty was all but annihilated, the Tyrells swore allegiance to the new king, Robert Baratheon.

Most recently, after the death of Robert Baratheon and the subsequent battles for rule of Westeros, the Tyrells allied themselves with Robert's charismatic youngest brother, Renly. They arranged for Renly to marry Margaery Tyrell, who would become queen if Renly succeeded and thus put Tyrell heirs on the Iron Throne. This hope was foiled when Renly was murdered, but the Tyrells adeptly shifted their marriage plans. Margaery arrived in King's Landing and, guided by her grandmother Lady Olenna Tyrell, usurped Sansa Stark as Joffrey's intended bride. Now, Margaery wages her own campaign to win over the people for the unpopular young King Joffrey.

[ABOVE] *The Tyrells watch a royal wedding that makes them grow even stronger.*
[OPPOSITE] *House Tyrell family tree.*

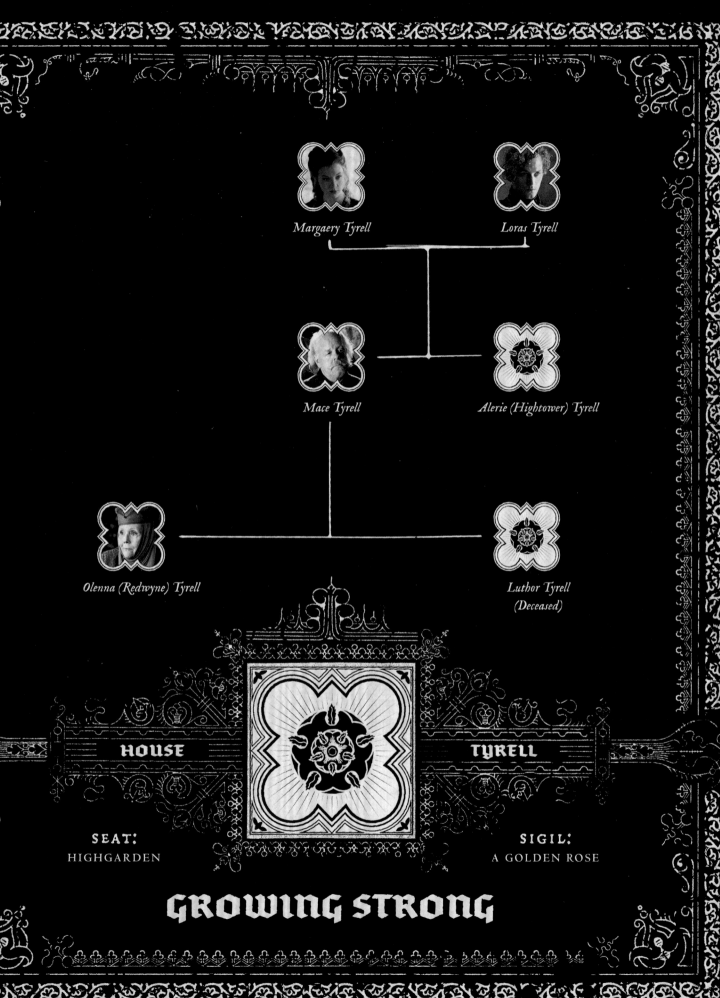

Margaery Tyrell

Loras Tyrell

Mace Tyrell

Alerie (Hightower) Tyrell

Olenna (Redwyne) Tyrell

Luthor Tyrell
(Deceased)

HOUSE TYRELL

SEAT:
HIGHGARDEN

SIGIL:
A GOLDEN ROSE

GROWING STRONG

OLENNA TYRELL

"THE WORLD IS OVERFLOWING WITH HORRIBLE THINGS, BUT THEY'RE ALL A TRAY OF CAKES NEXT TO DEATH."

—LADY OLENNA TYRELL

Lady Olenna Tyrell (Diana Rigg), known as the Queen of Thorns for the sting of her words, is the matriarch of the powerful Tyrell family and a masterful strategist. Sharp-tongued and keenly intelligent, she has little patience for idiocy and is rather disdainful of those she finds weak-witted. A superior player at court games, she has come to King's Landing to attend the wedding of her granddaughter Margaery Tyrell to King Joffrey and secure all possible advantages for House Tyrell. This includes encouraging Margaery's brother, Loras, to marry Sansa Stark, and thereby claim a strong foothold in the North for House Tyrell. Yet this attempt is thwarted by Tywin Lannister, who marries Sansa to Tyrion Lannister instead. Deeply mistrustful of everyone, Olenna's only true motivation is loyalty to her family.

DIANA RIGG (OLENNA TYRELL): I didn't know the books or the show before I met with David and Dan about Olenna, but I loved her immediately. She's just a ballsy old bag; she's subtle and witty and sophisticated and at the same time *so* brutal. I love all those mixtures. She's a tremendously strong woman, and I think that has to do with breeding. In my mind, she comes from a long, long line of strong women, and she just isn't daunted by many people. It's partly age as well—she's lived through a lot, survived more than most, and I think that makes her feel very strong.

CHARLES DANCE (TYWIN LANNISTER): Olenna is like the female Tywin Lannister. She's really the only one who can truly spar on the same level.

DAVID BENIOFF AND D. B. WEISS (CO-EXECUTIVE PRODUCERS AND WRITERS): Olenna is an iron lady in a man's world. She can't hold office or any title beyond "Lady," but that doesn't stop her from being the driving force behind the second most powerful family in the world. She's a spectacularly fun character to write for. At heart, both of us have always been tough seventy-year-old women.

The fact that Diana would grace us with her presence seemed unlikely. Then she agreed to meet us with Nina Gold for a drink in London. We asked her what she thought about it. She said, "An awful lot of bonking, isn't there? I love it." You can't put on presence like hers. She really is Olenna, only she is a tremendously sweet woman who, to our knowledge, has never had anyone killed.

[OPPOSITE] *The indomitable Lady Olenna (Diana Rigg).*
[ABOVE] *Two masters of strategy spar while walking the garden paths.*

HOUSE MARTELL:
A BRIEF HISTORY

"TELL YOUR FATHER I'M HERE. AND TELL HIM THE LANNISTERS AREN'T THE ONLY ONES WHO PAY THEIR DEBTS."

—OBERYN MARTELL

UNLIKE THE OTHER SIX KINGDOMS OF WESTEROS, Dorne was not conquered by Aegon Targaryen and his dragons. The Dornish denied Aegon a victory by using guerrilla tactics and pursuing a war of attrition in the desert. Ultimately, Aegon left Dorne without getting the Dornish to bend the knee. The Martells' pride over this is reflected in their sigil's words: "Unbowed, Unbent, Unbroken."

Many years before the Targaryen invasion, House Martell successfully united the bundle of conflicted Dornish states. Lord Mors Martell married Nymeria, a Rhoynar warrior queen, and the alliance of their forces was unstoppable. Afterward, Dorne adopted a number of Rhoynar customs, such as calling their rulers "princes" rather than "kings" and allowing the oldest child to inherit titles and lands regardless of gender. Eventually, House Martell allied with House Targaryen through marriage, and Dorne became one of the Seven Kingdoms of Westeros, while still retaining an unprecedented level of independence from the Iron Throne.

Sadly, not all such alliances in Westeros end so peacefully. Elia Martell was wed to Rhaegar Targaryen and bore him two beautiful children, but when Rhaegar abandoned his wife and kidnapped Lyanna Stark, Ned Stark's sister, it helped spark Robert's Rebellion, which ended in the overthrow of the Targaryen dynasty. During the final siege of King's Landing, Lannister forces raped and killed Elia and murdered her two children, the rumored actions of the Mountain. Afterward, House Martell withdrew from all alliances, left the capital, and nursed a deep mistrust and hatred of the Lannisters.

Fiercely independent, Dorne's support remains vital to the security of the crown. To help secure House Martell's support, Tywin Lannister arranged a marriage between Cersei's daughter Myrcella and one of the Dornish princes. In recent years, little has been seen from Dorne except its wine, but when the royal wedding between King Joffrey and Margaery Tyrell is announced, a Dornish delegation arrives in King's Landing to join the festivities and revisit unsettled scores. Elia's brother, the seductive and earthy prince Oberyn Martell, has decided this is an excellent opportunity to visit the capital, with an agenda all his own.

[ABOVE] *Tyrion and Bronn meet the Martell delegation.*
[OPPOSITE] *House Martell family tree.*

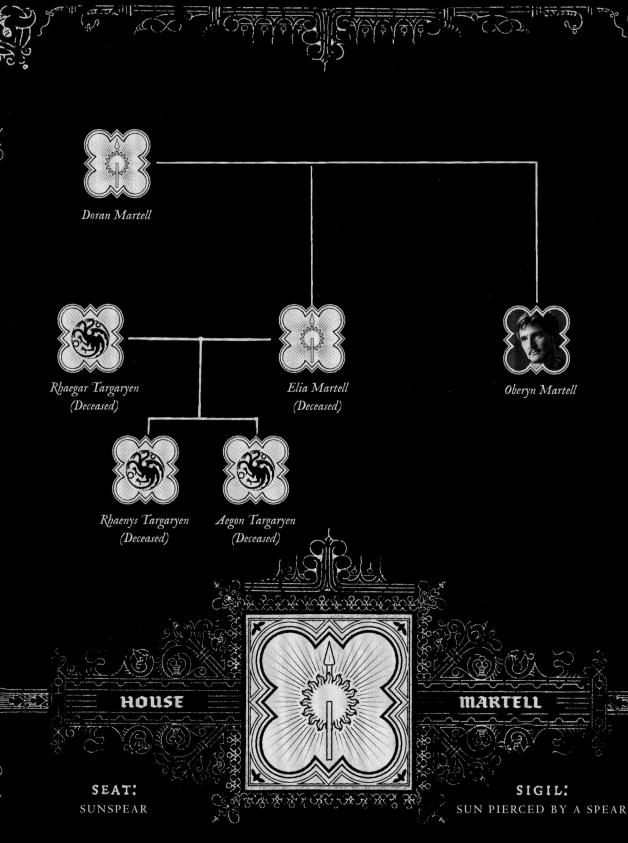

Doran Martell

Rhaegar Targaryen
(Deceased)

Elia Martell
(Deceased)

Oberyn Martell

Rhaenys Targaryen
(Deceased)

Aegon Targaryen
(Deceased)

HOUSE MARTELL

SEAT:
SUNSPEAR

SIGIL:
SUN PIERCED BY A SPEAR

UNBOWED, UNBENT, UNBROKEN

OBERYN MARTELL

"PEOPLE EVERYWHERE HAVE THEIR DIFFERENCES. IN SOME PLACES, THE HIGHBORN FROWN UPON THOSE OF LOW BIRTH. IN OTHER PLACES, THE RAPE AND MURDER OF WOMEN AND CHILDREN IS CONSIDERED DISTASTEFUL."

—OBERYN MARTELL

Oberyn Martell (Pedro Pascal) is the younger brother of the current Prince of Dorne, Doran Martell. A famed warrior, Oberyn is known as much for his lusty appetites as he is for his prowess in battle. He has fathered eight illegitimate daughters in Dorne, all of whom he loves and protects. Traveling with his bastard-born paramour Ellaria

Sand, Oberyn is ostensibly in King's Landing for the Royal Wedding, but he makes little secret of his true purpose: to discover the truth about the rape and murder of his sister Elia at the hands of the Mountain and, he suspects, on the orders of Tywin Lannister.

PEDRO PASCAL (OBERYN MARTELL): Coming onto an established show can be incredibly daunting, especially when you have to play someone as badass as Oberyn Martell. There were a lot of things to think about in terms of Oberyn's mind-set: living passionately, not caring about what anyone thinks or does, not compromising, having such a single focus and pursuing it relentlessly, while still somehow being a decent human being. He's a man that seems made of contradictions. He's driven by hate, but he's a great father and a loyal life partner. He's impulsive. He has a cold fury and a charm. He can seduce you or kill you. He's uncompromising and painfully honest. It's a decision he has made. He will not compromise on anything that he thinks or feels, and because of that he knows he won't live very long. It doesn't

make any sense to him to not live that way. It's not worth it to him.

ALEX GRAVES (DIRECTOR): The way I see the character, he's a hedonist because he's so tortured by what has happened. He's also a thorn in Tywin Lannister's side. He's a seriously dangerous guy. Pedro is so adorable and likeable; what he managed to do was humanize the character in such a significant way that it becomes even more interesting to watch.

[ABOVE] *Brute strength wins out over determination and grace as the Mountain and Oberyn Martell duel.* [OPPOSITE] *Oberyn Martell played by Pedro Pascal.*

— FINDING OBERYN —

Casting a show like Game of Thrones *has particular challenges. In the books, George R. R. Martin has created a world of vivid, immense detail, with extensive histories, exotic cultures, and unique characters. Finding the right actors to play each role requires fulfilling both the needs of the story as well as the imaginations of viewers.*

FRANK DOELGER (PRODUCER): David and Dan have written exceptional parts for actors, and Nina Gold's and Robert Sterne's taste is excellent, so we really were in a privileged position of just seeing the actors and deciding who fits in. We look at different acting styles and for the right look. Some actors seem quite modern, others are comfortably period. Some people are wonderful, but for some reason don't seem believable in this world. Others are perfect for the world, but don't have quite the right acting style—it's about bringing the right people into this beautiful world that has been created.

ROBERT STERNE (CASTING DIRECTOR): We knew that the character of Oberyn was the character event of the season. Part of his importance was that he was the introduction to an entirely new part of the world, namely Dorne. We knew that we were looking for someone Mediterranean, Egyptian, or South American who could fight and would really bring sensuality to the role.

PEDRO PASCAL (OBERYN MARTELL): When I got the audition, I felt it was an unobtainable gig. I was highly aware of the show and was completely up to date. For three seasons I allowed myself to be emotionally traumatized because I had to see what was going to happen to Joffrey. Then I get the audition sides and found out how and when he was going to die. I genuinely thought the fourth season was *ruined* for me.

I had filmed my first audition on my iPhone, and David and Dan wrote me this extremely generous and articulate email asking me to film it again to show a different color in Oberyn. I call it generous because they took the time to really communicate with someone they hadn't met, but who they thought *might* fit into their vision. So I taped it again—not on the iPhone this time! In my head, I was still a million miles away from getting the role. Eventually I was flown out to Belfast to meet with everyone. I took it as a good sign when I was going to stunt rehearsals and costume fittings when I arrived. It was only when it was made official that I dared tell anyone I got the part.

— COSTUMING DORNE —

In the southernmost region of Westeros lies the exotic and seductive kingdom known as Dorne. Made up of large expanses of mountains, stretches of vast desert, and rich coastal lands, Dorne is a kingdom of luxury and indulgence. The warmest climate on the continent inspires a very different feel to the highly constructed fashions of King's Landing.

MICHELE CLAPTON (COSTUME DESIGNER): The costumes for Oberyn Martell and Ellaria Sand are some of my favorites this season. The introduction of Dorne is something I've been waiting for, and I've been deliberately holding back on using their colors—the ochre yellow and the wonderful tans. We wanted them to have very distinctive looks; it's incredibly important to have those immediate visual cues to help you as the viewer. It was great to have these two characters lead into the next season, when we'll be going to Dorne and we'll have a chance to really push things creatively.

There are a lot of Indian influences, particularly with these fabrics. We sourced a lot of the fabric for the Dornish characters in India. I like the sand-washed silks, the weight of it and the depth of color.

Ellaria was an immensely interesting character to me. I think she moves a bit like a sidewinder—I always picture her disappearing over a dune or something. I liked the strength of her outfit, being able to lift the cape away to this very simple, sensual elegance, cut to the navel without revealing too much. It's a very assertive piece, both in movement and color. I love to think of what Cersei's reaction is when she sees it—after all, her daughter is now in Dorne.

Despite the substantial nature of some of the fabrics and the inclusion of metal sigils, Oberyn's costumes were in some ways quite feminine. There is something about the way that Pedro [Pascal] wore it, his masculinity, his total lack of fear of the feminine element, that made it so strong and deeply masculine on him.

His armor was one of my favorites of all the armors—the contrast between the weight of the Mountain's armor versus the lithe soft leather covering during the duel is visually exciting. Giampaolo [Grassi, the armor master,] and his assistants stamped all the leather with the design and hand cut all the elements. Being able to talk about it on the dummy, manipulate it around the shape of the body, the changes in the ratio of the symbols— it evolved in the workroom, and their input is immense. I think being part of that process leads to some of the most creative work. You can make replicas of Roman armor forever, and it can be beautiful, but it's not the same.

[ABOVE] *Costume designs for the Dornish.* [OPPOSITE TOP] *Oberyn and Ellaria adorned in the rich colors of the Dornish style.* [OPPOSITE BOTTOM LEFT] *Ellaria's costume realized.* [OPPOSITE BOTTOM RIGHT] *The influence of the desert snake scales can be seen in Oberyn's lightweight armor.*

— FILMING IN CROATIA —

Though filming in Northern Ireland can provide many things, the vast world that George R. R. Martin has created in Game of Thrones *includes an abundance of different environments—some of which require slightly better guaranteed climates. In previous years, parts of Westeros and Essos have been found in locations which included Malta and Morocco, but season four concentrated filming in just three countries: Iceland, Northern Ireland, and Croatia. Two cities in Croatia played significant roles: Dubrovnik hosted several scenes in King's Landing, providing the alleys Sansa escapes through, the site of the Royal Wedding, and the amphitheater for the fateful trial by combat between the Mountain and Oberyn Martell. The amphitheater set was built out of the remains of the famous Hotel Belvedere, which was heavily shelled during battles that took place in October 1991. Farther north, the city of Split stood in for Meereen, the slave city that becomes Daenerys's latest conquest, an entirely new location for the* Game of Thrones *team.*

DUNCAN MUGGOCH (UK PRODUCTION MANAGER): Working with Embassy Films in Croatia is extremely helpful. For much of the Croatian crew, working on the show is more of a summer job—the film production industry is still in its infancy. There is a core group of professional film people that work on everything. The logistics of filming in some of the locations are incredibly complex—250 people arriving with trucks in a city that isn't built for it can cause chaos. Dubrovnik is such a beautiful city. They are very welcoming. I give [line producer] Erika Milutin a huge amount of credit for that.

Of all our locations, I'm thrilled with the way the amphitheater turned out—it began as a bombed-out, 1970s, graffiti-filled hotel overlooking the bay and became something unrecognizable.

Split had its own challenges. The city was not a place that had experienced filming on anything like our scale before. Finding things like caterers was something of a challenge. There is no extras agency, but we were able to do everything within the company. We had open calls and trawled the streets for people who might fit the more particular requirements, like the Unsullied. There is such a passion that surrounds the show that many people traveled to Croatia to be involved. It was quite an international crowd in the end.

DEB RILEY (PRODUCTION DESIGNER): When we discovered the city of Split, and more particularly the Fortress at Klis, it really informed the design of Meereen in a way that I'm not sure could have been achieved through just books and trawling the Internet. Klis gave us just enough architecture to build around it and create Meereen.

With Dubrovnik there is a very particular look that is resonant of King's Landing and that is clear in previous scenes. When we traveled north to Split, there was a feeling that this could be the basis for Meereen: there was a different color to the rock. There was a beautiful organic nature to it, with wild sage growing out from the brick.

[OPPOSITE] *Sansa escapes from King's Landing.* [ABOVE] *Hotel Belvedere transformed into the dueling arena.* [FOLLOWING SPREAD] *The unknowing delivery of a poisoned chalice.*

— THE DEATH OF JOFFREY —
EPISODE 402: "THE LION AND THE ROSE"

"A ROYAL WEDDING IS NOT AN AMUSEMENT. A ROYAL WEDDING IS HISTORY."

—KING JOFFREY

With the royal wedding between King Joffrey Baratheon and Margaery Tyrell, a new alliance is formed that promises to finally bring lasting security to King's Landing. Tywin Lannister and Lady Olenna Tyrell have gotten their way, and all seems well. The wedding participants leave the Sept of Baelor to join the crowds of guests for a celebratory feast of epic proportions.

Yet Joffrey's pleasure often rests in others' pain, and at the feast he hosts a spectacle designed to humiliate both his former fiancée Sansa Stark and his uncle Tyrion. A troupe of performing dwarves burst through the lion's head stage and reenact the War of the Five Kings and the death of Robb Stark in the most vulgar fashion. Joffrey also demands that Tyrion, antagonized beyond reason, service him as a cupbearer, but timing is everything. Secretly poisoned by his drink, Joffrey begins to choke, dying in agony before the horrified crowd and his stunned family.

In the confusion of Joffrey's death, Sansa escapes with Ser Dontos, a man she believes she can trust, unaware that her flight makes her appear guilty of murder. Tyrion, too shocked to move, is immediately seized for regicide at the command of an hysterical Cersei.

JACK GLEESON (JOFFREY BARATHEON): There is no question that Joffrey had to die in a way that was something like this. He can't just fall off a ladder and go splat. The audience needs and also really *deserves* a nice drawn out choking death. It's the most painful way one can imagine to die, and it's shown in a very visceral way, so it offers something of a catharsis for all the years of Joffrey that have come before.

PETER DINKLAGE (TYRION LANNISTER): When Joffrey dies, it is the worst possible timing for Tyrion. The wedding celebrations begin with a humiliating pageant, and then Joffrey is killed. I honestly don't think Tyrion saw either coming, however much he might have hoped for the latter.

LENA HEADEY (CERSEI LANNISTER): Even before Joffrey dies, Cersei's world is beginning to crumble. She began the series as an invincible force, married to the king and very much in control. That has begun to shift. She's hugely threatened by Margaery, this beautiful young girl who is taking Joffrey's attention. She knows she is losing her grasp on him. He can't really be controlled. When he dies, Cersei comes apart in a way you would never expect. It's the beginning of a descent into madness. Being a parent

is both a gift and a curse—there is no love like that of a parent for their child. You open yourself to something extraordinary. When I was lying over his body, I was thinking of the loss of no longer having *Jack* around—this warm, funny, intelligent being, so beyond me in wisdom. I couldn't look at him on the day without tearing up. Cersei was Joffrey's one true ally, and he never saw it. Now she's completely alone.

NIKOLAJ COSTER-WALDAU (JAIME LANNISTER): Cersei's reaction is that of a mother who has lost her son. Jaime's isn't. I don't believe Jaime has ever had that connection with Joffrey. He's never been blind to what sort of person Joffrey is. His reaction is for *her*. There is no love lost.

BRYAN COGMAN (CO-PRODUCER AND WRITER): Cersei has devoted her entire life to the advancement and protection of her children, particularly first-born Joffrey. I love the way Lena played the scene—but it's consistent with how she's always played Cersei. She's never a villain, never the ice queen. She's a flesh-and-blood person who loves her family and feels the same all-consuming grief at losing Joffrey that a "heroic" character like Catelyn felt at losing Robb.

PETER DINKLAGE (TYRION LANNISTER): Cersei truly believes Tyrion was guilty; there is no question. She loves her children so much. She is a true scorpion to defend them. The madness

that comes with it makes sense. The instant she believes it, she is pure venom. Everyone else is simply following the big fat liar that is Tyrion's father.

DAVID BENIOFF AND D. B. WEISS (CO-EXECUTIVE PRODUCERS AND WRITERS): Although Joffrey's death was indeed grotesque, it wasn't meant to be triumphant. We knew many people would take it that way, but it's not played as a victory. If we'd ended the episode on Joffrey's death, it might have, but the accusatory fingers point right at Tyrion before we have time to savor Joffrey's demise. For Joffrey's final moments, Jack and Lena stripped their characters down to the bone—he was a son in trouble begging his mother for help, and she was the mother who couldn't help her son when he needed her most. Something definitely snaps in Cersei at this moment—her "anger" phase kicks in right away, and hits Tyrion head-on.

JACK GLEESON (JOFFREY BARATHEON): In terms of the experience, the run up to my death was great fun to do. The actual death was very technical—we had different stages of makeup, and everything had to be shot repeatedly, so it was a little harder to do. For me, though, it was wonderful to be able to do my final scenes with so many of the cast around me, just to be able to see them all before I went.

[OPPOSITE] *Concept art for the Sept of Baelor dressed for the wedding.*
[ABOVE] *With his dying breath, Joffrey makes an accusation.*

— COSTUMING MARGAERY —

MICHELE CLAPTON (COSTUME DESIGNER): Margaery's wedding dress is actually quite a traditional dress. Unlike Sansa, who is being forced into something and feels quite oppressed, this is a wedding Margaery wants. She knows the power she will gain despite the fact that she is marrying someone grotesque. It's quite demure so as to appeal to people, but her sigil is all over the dress. I wanted to capture the idea of the twisting and strangling and taking over of the Lannisters. Even Joffrey's wedding crown has elements of that, with the Baratheon elements being overtaken by the roses. It looks beautiful and soft from a distance; it's only when you look at the details that you realize it is covered in thorns and is not at all what it seems.

The dress is made of silk linen printed with a beautiful pattern of leaves and a two-tone gray feel that gives it a steely edge. The embroidery was done by Michele [Carragher], who has a wonderful organic sensibility. At times it would get too heavy, so we would pull it back and remove elements, or it would go too far the other way and be too pretty. We adjusted until we found the right balance. I then decided that the roses should be added to the train. I really had no idea how many would be needed.

MICHELE CARRAGHER (EMBROIDERER): It all begins with Michele's sketches. We discussed at length how it couldn't just be pretty, it really needed to have this harder edge. For the dress

I made over 350 individual roses by hand for the back of the skirt and train. I could do one in about ten minutes, which meant that it took about sixty hours in total to do them all. The stems were made from a metallic cord that was then covered in an Italian mesh wire to create the thickness needed. The thorns were a combination of Czech glass spikes and hand-folded leather that was painted silver to match the scheme. Some of the more delicate branches were also leather, braided and hand-finished in the same silver. Each of the leaves were made of velvet, cut and individually placed. From start to finish, the detailing on the dress took about ten days to complete.

MICHELE CLAPTON (COSTUME DESIGNER): When I saw that there were steps in the shot, I was worried that the skirts would end up bouncing and looking too theatrical—the skirt was bowed slightly to give a lift to the design. But in the end it lay beautifully because of the weight in the train. Director Alex Graves said it was the only time he had ever changed a shot for a costume— to capture it as Margaery ascended.

[OPPOSITE] *The royal couple dressed in full regalia.* [ABOVE] *The wedding dress complete with details reflecting the elegant power and vicious prick of the Tyrell sigil.*

SHAE

"MEN ONLY WANT ONE THING FROM A PRETTY GIRL."

—SHAE

A skilled and charming prostitute, Shae (Sibel Kekilli) does not share her secrets easily. She has learned the hard way to be careful of whom she trusts. The ambitious Shae becomes the singular companion of Tyrion Lannister, traveling with him to King's Landing in secret when he is named Hand of the King. In order to protect her identity from Cersei Lannister, Tyrion arranges for Shae to become Sansa Stark's handmaiden in the castle. Shae and Sansa become close, and Shae tries to protect her from both herself and her enemies. Shae is no stranger to the games that people like to play with innocent young girls.

Tyrion is deeply in love with Shae, but he constantly fears for her safety. Tyrion tries to send her away repeatedly, before the Battle of Blackwater and later when he realizes he will be trapped in a marriage to Sansa. Angered by Tyrion's acquiescence to his father's machinations, Shae becomes jealous of Sansa. Increasingly erratic and confrontational, Shae begins to doubt if Tyrion ever truly loved her at all.

SIBEL KEKILLI (SHAE): I love the character of Shae. She's a very complicated young woman who hasn't had an easy life, but she is smart. If she wasn't clever, she would never have found herself as the companion to Tyrion. In the beginning, maybe there was a strategy to it; it was a job to be with Tyrion. She's been hurt a lot, and it's only when she begins to trust him that she begins to love him. She was prepared to risk her life to be with him. She never would have betrayed him the way she did at the trial if she didn't have deep feelings. Hate and love are so close in so many ways. When he was so dishonest at the end, even though he was trying to protect her, she knows he is lying. When he calls her "whore," I think it truly breaks her heart. That is the moment that she truly begins to hate.

PETER DINKLAGE (TYRION LANNISTER): He's fallen in love with Shae, and that's his vulnerability. I don't think Tyrion had ever truly been vulnerable until he met this woman. I love that David and Dan expanded on her character because I think it shows a different side to him when he is with her. Everyone needs to have their own kryptonite. She needs constant protection to hide her identity and their relationship, and he goes to great lengths to do that. I don't think he would do that for much else, other than to perhaps protect his own life. It's made him weak in a way, and he hates it.

[ABOVE] *There is nothing more dangerous than a woman with a broken heart.*
[OPPOSITE] *Jaime must get to grips with having a new, inferior sword hand.*
[FOLLOWING SPREAD] *Cersei and Jaime try and relearn each other.*

JAIME LANNISTER RETURNS

*"MY BLOODY HONOR IS BEYOND REPAIR. BUT THE ANSWER IS STILL NO. I DON'T WANT
CASTERLY ROCK. I DON'T WANT A WIFE. I DON'T WANT CHILDREN."*

—JAIME LANNISTER

Jaime Lannister (Nikolaj Coster-Waldau) returns to King's Landing a changed man. Everything—being captured twice, the loss of his hand, his time on the road with Brienne (Gwendoline Christie)—has affected Jaime. Having always been known as the Kingslayer, a great warrior, and a Lannister, Jaime is reluctantly questioning what he believes about himself. While Brienne confronts him over the promises he's made, which represent who he's become, Jaime really only has one goal in mind—to reunite with his sister the way they once were.

Yet Cersei (Lena Headey) has changed as well. Her feelings for Jaime are conflicted; she feels deserted by him, and now he's returned wounded, in her mind a lesser man than before. Further, Tywin wants Jaime to quit the Kingsguard and take up control of Casterly Rock, the Lannister stronghold, to continue the family legacy. Instead Jaime refuses, deciding to remain in the Kingsguard, and in King's Landing, in order to be close to Cersei and in doing so faces a new reality: disowned by his father, repulsive to his lover, a one-handed warrior with no claim to his old skill as a fighter. Who is he now?

NIKOLAJ COSTER-WALDAU (JAIME LANNISTER): I think there is part of Jaime that wants to pretend that nothing has changed, and that when he returns to King's Landing, it will go back to the way it was. There is a moment with Brienne when she confronts him about his promises, and he just wants her to leave him to return to his life, but he knows he can't.

GWENDOLINE CHRISTIE (BRIENNE OF TARTH): There is this thing in Shakespeare that when people go into the woods, it's often symbolic of confusion. This to me feels like that—they go off together to find themselves. I think it's very brave of Brienne to remind Jaime of his promises, but she's also reminding him of their relationship, this friendship they developed. It's a hard thing to be that open, but his acknowledgment of his promises and then endowing them with physical form [her armor] is incredibly symbolic. It shows his acceptance of who she is as a woman and the trust he has in her as a warrior.

NIKOLAJ COSTER-WALDAU (JAIME LANNISTER): Sometimes you hear these stories of great trauma, or in this case the loss of his mastery of swords, and the loss of his hand. I think that forced him to find who he is. I think his understanding of people and morality has been there all along, but the situation is dragging it out of him. He also knows that his sister is not how he wants her to be—it's like she's revolted by him, and the gift of the gold hand is an attempt to make him whole again. There's something quite *wrong* in that. Her outrage at his leaving shows their relationship is very one-sided. It's about her needs, about when she can fit him into her life. I think he finds it unfair, but accepts it. It's how they've always been.

LENA HEADEY (CERSEI LANNISTER): I know Jaime loves Cersei. I question if she loves him, or if she finds a safety in him. I have always maintained that she really would like to *be* him, to have the freedom to fight. She believes she is smarter, but she is confined by being a woman. I think that, missing the part that she probably admired most in terms of what his sword hand represented—his sexuality, his strength—that is where envy lay, and now it's gone. She doesn't like his vulnerability.

TYRION ON TRIAL

"I DIDN'T KILL JOFFREY, BUT I WISH I HAD. WATCHING YOUR VICIOUS BASTARD DIE GAVE ME MORE RELIEF THAN A THOUSAND LYING WHORES."

—TYRION LANNISTER

Tyrion Lannister has always known his father hated him, but even he is surprised to be accused of Joffrey's murder by his own sister and put on public trial for a crime he did not commit. However, Cersei, seemingly mad with grief, is intent on destroying her brother for murdering her son.

Tywin Lannister sees this as an opportunity to rid himself of the son he despises. Meanwhile, Tywin also uses Tyrion's life as a way to control Jaime and force him to accept the role of Lord of Casterly Rock. Jaime Lannister is caught between loyalty to a brother he knows to be innocent and feelings for a sister whom he still loves beyond reason. Since he can't stop the proceedings, he agrees to Tywin's terms in exchange for a promise of Tyrion's safety.

During the trial, in a court full of sycophants and secret agendas, witness after false witness stands to accuse Tyrion of malevolent intent, and he begins to realize his life is in true danger. Worst of all, the woman he truly adores—Shae—betrays him and lies to the court. Her testimony sends Tyrion over the edge, and in a moment of pure rage, he throws away the deal that would see him banished to the Wall and leaves his fate in the hands of the gods.

This contest would be unwinnable, except that Oberyn Martell agrees to fight on Tyrion's behalf. Oberyn is less interested in saving Tyrion than in fulfilling his own desire—to learn the truth about the murder of his sister and to kill the Mountain. In this, Oberyn succeeds just before the Mountain returns the favor.

DAVID BENIOFF AND D. B. WEISS (CO-EXECUTIVE PRODUCERS AND WRITERS): Tyrion is watching all the contempt of his father and sister—and all the anger he's thrown back at them in turn—come home to roost. For something he didn't do. On some level, he's too worldly to dwell much on the fact that he's innocent. But on a deeper level, the fact that his own family wants to have him executed for something he didn't do . . . it cuts him deep, as the end of the season proves.

BRYAN COGMAN (CO-PRODUCER AND WRITER): Writing the trial sequence was a lot of fun and hugely challenging. I got to play with all the tropes of the classic "courtroom drama,"

but I had to be careful it didn't seem anachronistic or turn into a spoof. The trap was creating *Law and Order: Westeros*. We made the decision to make the case against Tyrion largely based on actual events that happened on the show (with one or two exceptions), albeit distorted by Cersei to make Tyrion seem guilty of Joffrey's murder. But, in the end, the trial theatrics and plot are secondary to the fact that this long sequence is essentially a scene between the Lannister kids and their father—a scene that exists almost entirely in the looks and reactions between them and the family history boiling under the surface. Director Alik Sakharov was particularly mindful of this—getting tons of reaction shots from Peter, Nikolaj, Lena, and Charles that really end up being the spine of the sequence. Peter is extraordinary in that scene—he finally can't take it anymore and lets his father and the people of King's Landing know what he really thinks of them. "I am guilty of being a dwarf!" is such a powerful statement—a terrific line of George's taken directly from the book.

CHARLES DANCE (TYWIN LANNISTER): I've gotten quite used to the way Tywin behaves now. What I've realized is that he will genuinely stop at nothing to reach his goals. As time has gone on I have wondered if there is a tiny moment of regret in that, but that little element is just a color. That's all. The people he recruits for the trial to sit in judgment are those he has chosen as puppets. He doesn't think Tyrion is guilty, but he wants him out, and this is convenient.

NIKOLAJ COSTER-WALDAU (JAIME LANNISTER): In my mind, it's quite simple. If Jaime thought Tyrion had killed Joffrey, he might understand his sister's utter obsession with killing their brother, but he knows Tyrion didn't do it. He thinks she's playing two games at the same time—she's hurt and grief stricken, but I'm not sure he really thinks she truly believes it. He suspects it's about control of the kingdom by getting Tyrion out completely, leaving only Jaime and her father.

LENA HEADEY (CERSEI LANNISTER): In that moment when Joffrey dies, there is no question at all in my mind that Cersei believes Tyrion is guilty. If she were able to open herself up to the reality of how others saw Joffrey, it might be different, but in her mind it's completely logical. The trial is her only point of sanity now. If she can lynch him, if she can cause him pain, she might find some peace again. She's taken everything she has left and is focused on one single goal. To destroy Tyrion, she's prepared to even destroy herself. She holds him responsible for everything, the death of her mother and sending Myrcella away, and she wants to hurt him. The fact that Jaime, the man she trusts the *most*, will not take her side is a betrayal that leaves her completely alone in King's Landing.

PETER DINKLAGE (TYRION LANNISTER): Everything up until the moment in which Shae arrives is fully expected by Tyrion. He knows exactly how everyone is going to behave. He's smarter than them.

Before the trial began, Tyrion tried to save Shae by sending her away and making her believe that he did not care. He was prepared to sacrifice his own happiness to save her. As the season went on, I thought a lot about people who feel entitled to certain things, and Tyrion certainly feels entitled to his birthright as a Lannister, but I'm not sure he feels like he's entitled to be loved. It's incredibly sad, but I just don't think he knows how to fight for her.

When Shae stands before him and betrays everything, lying to the court, it's a game changer. He didn't think she was capable of it. When it comes down to it, that's the moment when it all becomes a nightmare for Tyrion. When he starts to talk about what he's really on trial for, it's because of Shae. He has nothing to lose; he's screwed either way, so there is a release there. It's interesting, though, because no one seems to think it's anything other than the little man ranting, apart from Oberyn. He's the only one who leans in to take notice.

PEDRO PASCAL (OBERYN MARTELL): My first scene ever on *Game of Thrones* was in a cell with Peter Dinklage, agreeing to fight for Tyrion in the trial by combat against the Mountain. It was very much a baptism of fire. Oberyn shouldn't really be standing for a Lannister, but there is something in Tyrion that Oberyn respects. Despite his name, Tyrion is a man who was born with nothing in his favor, and Oberyn sees something of a kindred spirit in him. Ultimately, though, what this choice comes down to is a chance to get to the Mountain, who for Oberyn has always been the target. He's completely driven by hate, but unlike Cersei, he's not blinded by it. He can see that Tyrion is someone who transcends his family name, or social convention, and despite his disadvantages is more courageous than everyone around him. Being able to save a man like Tyrion is an added bonus to him.

PETER DINKLAGE (TYRION LANNISTER): When the Mountain finds the strength to kill Oberyn, it looks very much like all hope is lost. It's the end in many ways. For sure it is the darkest moment in his life so far, but Tyrion hasn't lived so long without finding a glimmer of hope. I wonder if even in that moment he knows that Jaime will come through for him.

PEDRO PASCAL (OBERYN MARTELL): Dying was different for me on *Game of Thrones*. I've been killed before, and I think it's kind of cool, but with this I couldn't disassociate from what it meant in the narrative, which has never happened to me before. I couldn't let go of Oberyn being on this journey to avenge his sister and her children—how emotionally brutal it was for someone so elegant and good to go down like that. It was horrifying to listen to Ellaria scream the way she did. It's the absolute embodiment of the pain of that moment.

[OPPOSITE] *The judges sit for the trial of Tyrion Lannister.*

— ESCAPE OF TYRION LANNISTER —
EPISODE 410: "THE CHILDREN"

"TRUST ME, MY FRIEND. I'VE BROUGHT YOU THIS FAR."

—VARYS

Nothing goes according to plan during Tyrion's trial by combat. The Mountain, near death and made to confess to the heinous crimes that Oberyn Martell accuses him of, still manages to kill Oberyn. As the last echoes of Ellaria Sand's screams fade in the arena, Tywin Lannister sentences his own son to death, and Tyrion is returned to the cells to await execution.

Jaime Lannister, however, is unable to stomach the thought of his own brother being put to death for a crime he had no part in. Jaime arranges with Varys to smuggle Tyrion out of the country

and over the Narrow Sea to Essos. Rather than fleeing immediately, though, Tyrion seeks out his father's chambers first. There, he finds Shae, whose presence makes clear that her betrayal of Tyrion is complete. They fight, and in their struggle, Tyrion kills Shae. Shocked at what he's done, and boiling over with emotion, Tyrion next finds and kills Tywin in a way, and place, each least expects.

[ABOVE] *Jaime leads Tyrion to his escape.*
[OPPOSITE] *Tyrion finds himself at a crossroads.*

ALEX GRAVES (DIRECTOR): We had a long rehearsal before shooting Tyrion and Shae because I didn't want anyone getting hurt. I also hadn't found the way of expressing the awfulness of this situation for them both. It started with Tyrion on top of Shae and choking her, but then I came up with the idea of Tyrion falling off the bed and not letting go. It was incredible, with Sibel finding the perfect way to be pulled back. It just came together into something perfectly *terrible*.

PETER DINKLAGE (TYRION LANNISTER): The way that the killing of Shae is written is how I think violence happens in real life, actually. She had a knife and would have killed him—it just happens so quickly, and then someone is dead, and no one really knows how it happened. He's not really apologizing for killing her so much as for bringing her into the world at all. Realistically, how long was a relationship with his father going to last before Cersei got her or something? She would have survived the world outside the Lannisters, for sure. But he knew that the day he met her and brought her into this horrible community of people, from that moment she was doomed.

SIBEL KEKILLI (SHAE): There is definitely something deliberate in Shae's choice to be with Tywin. He's the most powerful man she can be with, but he is also Tyrion's father. It is the worst thing she could do to him. In those last moments, when Tyrion discovers her in Tywin's bed, there is such a feeling of sadness and shame. They both seem so vulnerable in that moment. Going for the knife almost seems like a reflex to me. When he starts to strangle her, she fights, but then there is almost a moment of acceptance. It feels like a loss to me—that they could have been happy if they had just been left alone.

PETER DINKLAGE (TYRION LANNISTER): In that moment, when Jaime sets Tyrion free and he goes the other way from freedom, I don't think he has any intention of killing his father. David [Benioff] and Dan [Weiss] feel differently, but in my mind, it's actually a very pure moment. It's only after he's killed Shae that he finds the crossbow, and in that second he needs to hear the truth from his father. That's all he needs. I hate the word, but he needs *closure* on the situation.

CHARLES DANCE (TYWIN LANNISTER): I've loved working on the show. In a way I wish it wasn't so soon, but Tywin always had to go in a spectacular way. It was so right for his end. House Lannister has sort of imploded in on itself this season. I think people will miss Tywin after he's dead and gone, but they will revel in how he goes.

ALEX GRAVES (DIRECTOR): After the death of Shae, I think Tyrion's gone a little mad. I never felt comfortable with the idea that he could kill a woman he loved that much. I wanted there to be the long hallway we could follow Tyrion down to really bring out the idea that whoever he ran into was going to be in very serious trouble. I was really unsure of how finding Tywin in the toilet was going to play dramatically. It's so uncomfortable visually, but you are also looking at someone who does not really know what they are dealing with. In the end, I wanted to focus on the intensity of their relationship by shooting closely in on their faces—to catch every look in the eye.

PETER DINKLAGE (TYRION LANNISTER): There's nothing dignified in Tywin's death. I think it's perfect. He couldn't die on a battlefield because he's too good. He'd never die of a broken heart; he's too cold. It's just perfect. It's the only place he's vulnerable, but what was amazing was there was no trace of embarrassment in the performance. It was just Tywin, dealing with what was being presented to him. It was Charles's last scene of the entire series, so it had a certain tragic sadness to it. I will miss working with Charles, he is quite simply one of the best actors I have ever worked with.

DAVID BENIOFF AND D. B. WEISS (CO-EXECUTIVE PRODUCERS AND WRITERS): Tyrion has been sitting in his cell, helpless, almost certainly thinking futile thoughts about murdering the father who's letting him fester there . . . but the actual decision to kill Tywin has to happen in the moment, since the opportunity comes upon him so quickly and unexpectedly. It's a disastrous move in so many ways . . . but Tyrion definitely has an impulsive streak. Murder is often an impulsive action, of course. But it's equally true that this particular impulse has been building in him for a long time.

We'll have to see where he picks up in season five . . . but these murders definitely break something in him. These two people defined him in so many ways, for good and for ill. Killing them is like killing large pieces of himself.

Charles Dance was one of the three actors we knew we wanted from the moment we finished George's first book (the other two were Peter Dinklage and Sean Bean). His death creates such a void in the world of the show. He may not have hesitated in making unpopular decisions . . . but wait to see what happens when the one guy who was truly in charge isn't around anymore. We will miss Charles terribly.

[OPPOSITE] *The most powerful man in Westeros is brought to an undignified end.*

Part Six

ON THE ROAD

"You know what kind of stories poor men love the most? Ones about rich girls they'll never meet."

— LITTLEFINGER

JAIME LANNISTER AND BRIENNE OF TARTH MAY HAVE RETURNED TO KING'S LANDING, BUT THE ROADS OF WESTEROS REMAIN BUSY WITH THE COMINGS AND GOINGS OF TRAVELERS WHOSE MISSIONS ARE AS DIFFERENT AS THEIR DESTINATIONS.

HAVING SUCCESSFULLY WON THE NORTH THROUGH TREACHERY, ROOSE BOLTON RETURNS HOME TO THE DREADFORT TO DISCOVER RAMSAY HAS BEEN BUSY IN HIS ABSENCE. THOUGH ANY ATTEMPT HAS SO FAR FAILED TO FORCE BALON GREYJOY TO RELINQUISH HIS HOLD ON MOAT CAITLIN, THAT MAY CHANGE WITH THE HELP OF RAMSAY'S NEWEST CREATION, THE BROKEN AND PITEOUS CAPTIVE REEK.

SANSA STARK HAS FINALLY ESCAPED KING'S LANDING AND FOUND REFUGE IN THE EYRIE UNDER THE PROTECTION OF HER AUNT, LYSA ARRYN. BUT HER FATE STILL FEELS TENUOUS. SANSA MUST HIDE HER IDENTITY FOR HER OWN PROTECTION, AND SHE AGAIN FINDS HERSELF UNDER THE CONTROL OF A MAN WHOSE INTENTIONS SHE DOES NOT TRUST, THE SCHEMING LITTLEFINGER, UNLESS SANSA CAN TURN THE TABLES.

FOR ARYA STARK, HER NARROW ESCAPE FROM THE RED WEDDING HAS ONLY REINFORCED HER DESIRE FOR VENGEANCE. AN UNWILLING CAPTIVE OF THE BRUTISH MERCENARY THE HOUND, ARYA NEVERTHELESS DISCOVERS THAT, IF SHE WANTS TO LEARN ABOUT KILLING, SHE NOW HAS THE BEST POSSIBLE TUTOR.

HOUSE BOLTON:
A BRIEF HISTORY

"WE'VE BEEN FLAYING OUR ENEMIES FOR A THOUSAND YEARS."

—RAMSAY SNOW

AS ONE OF THE OLDEST AND MOST POWERFUL HOUSES IN THE NORTH, House Bolton gained a reputation for brutality with their custom of flaying the skins from their enemies and displaying them within the Dreadfort, the fortress that is their house seat. Rumors abound that some even wore the skins as cloaks.

For centuries the Boltons were the main rivals of the Starks for control of the North. Then, a thousand years ago, Harlon Stark crushed a Bolton revolt by pursuing a two-year siege of the Dreadfort. Afterward, the Boltons swore to renounce their practice of flaying, and they remained loyal bannermen of the Starks. That is, until Roose Bolton betrayed Robb Stark at the Red Wedding and allied himself with the Lannisters. Now, as Warden of the North, Roose controls Winterfell, and with the help of his bastard son, Ramsay Snow, he is trying to solidify House Bolton's rule over the North.

While the Boltons may have claimed the title of Warden from the fallen House Stark, control remains far from absolute.

Balon Greyjoy claimed the title of King of the Iron Islands, and his forces retain control over the key strategic hold of Moat Cailin, barring free passage from the South. The Iron Islanders are legendary for their resilience, and the skills of their fighters would likely cost House Bolton men it cannot afford to lose, posing a dilemma for the new Warden and a challenge for his son.

For Ramsay, it is the opportunity he has been waiting all his life for—to gain his father's approval and his claim to the name Bolton. After months of manipulation and torture, he has broken Theon Greyjoy down to a mere puppet—a pitiful creature known as Reek. When the opportunity arises to use his new plaything in a twisted Trojan horse strategy with the besieged Ironborn at Moat Cailin, he tests Reek's loyalty by having him "play" Theon and deny his identity all at once.

[PREVIOUS SPREAD] *Sansa's covert arrival at the Eyrie.*
[ABOVE] *Ramsay leads the Bolton bannermen.* [OPPOSITE] *House Bolton family tree.*

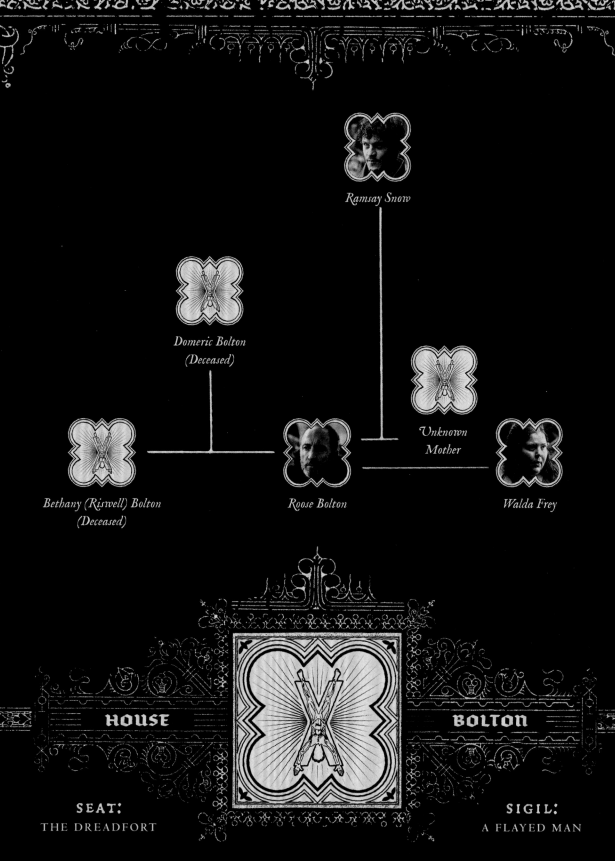

Ramsay Snow

Domeric Bolton
(Deceased)

Unknown
Mother

Bethany (Ryswell) Bolton
(Deceased)

Roose Bolton

Walda Frey

HOUSE   BOLTON

SEAT: SIGIL:
THE DREADFORT   A FLAYED MAN

OUR BLADES ARE SHARP

— CREATING DARK SANSA —

> "THE FIRST TIME I SAW YOU, YOU WERE JUST A CHILD. A GIRL FROM THE NORTH,
> COME TO THE CAPITAL FOR THE FIRST TIME. YOU'RE NOT A CHILD ANYMORE."
>
> —PETYR BAELISH

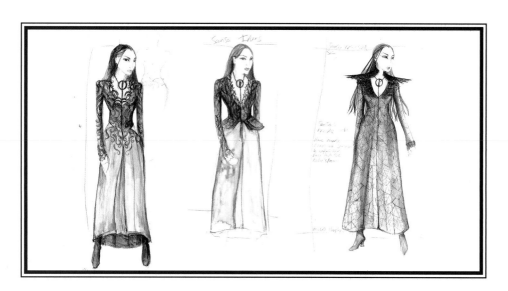

Implicated in the murder of King Joffrey, Sansa Stark (Sophie Turner) escapes the hell of King's Landing in the company of potentially the most dangerous man she has ever met—Petyr Baelish, or Littlefinger, a man with unclear motives but obvious ambition. Littlefinger once loved Sansa's mother and claimed to love Sansa's Aunt Lysa—that is, until he threw her to her death for attacking Sansa in a fit of jealous rage. As the only witness to the crime, Sansa must make a choice—does she allow herself to become a pawn in another man's game, or does she apply the lessons learned in the Machiavellian world of King's Landing and become a player herself? After successfully manipulating the hearing that would have condemned Baelish and beginning to take control of the Vale through her cousin, Sansa takes on a dramatic new look to reflect her new attitude.

SOPHIE TURNER (SANSA STARK): Sansa has always had an inner strength, but she has been so oppressed for the last three seasons. She has had very little say in her own life. I think that is what makes her decide that the time has come to make her own decisions and to be her own person, rather than to be confined to other people's expectations of who she should be. It's a very nice moment when the new look is revealed, and you realize she is a force to be reckoned with. It is the perfect representation of how much other people have underestimated both her strength and intelligence.

MICHELE CLAPTON (COSTUME DESIGNER): David and Dan came to me with the idea of a transformation for Sansa. They wanted her to be her own woman rather than this victim. I loved the idea, but I wasn't sure how to go about getting there. I hate that fantasy thing where things magically appear. The dress had to be something that could have been adapted from something she already owned, using materials she had access to. So the shape is not radically different. If she's dying her hair, she can dye some fabric. It's meant to be as if she is somewhat reborn while mourning for all that she has lost. We know that she has the skill because we have seen her doing needlework from season one, but I liked the idea that after this, she doesn't want to sew anymore. The metal piece is really a miniature of Arya's sword, Needle, and the idea is that there's a ring that you stitch through and then that's her weapon. I like that she carries it when she descends the stairs; now she's armed and it's a link to her family.

It's so easy to make someone look strong, but if you don't think about the story, it's sort of a wasted gesture. She could have probably looked even more amazing if I had put the reasoned arguments of where it could have come from aside, but ultimately, it makes it a stronger look if it's a more believable transition.

[ABOVE] *Costume designs for the new Dark Sansa.* [OPPOSITE] *A newly born warrior chooses her outer armor.* [FOLLOWING SPREAD] *Sansa is reminded to never believe in safety won too easily.*

ARYA AND THE HOUND

"HATE'S AS GOOD A THING AS ANY TO KEEP A PERSON GOING. BETTER THAN MOST."

—THE HOUND

Since their escape from the Brotherhood Without Banners, Arya Stark (Maisie Williams) has been an unwilling captive of Sandor Clegane, the Hound (Rory McCann). The dynamic between the brutal warrior and the young fugitive changes after they witness the carnage of the Red Wedding, and the Hound becomes determined to take Arya to Lysa Arryn at the Eyrie, hundreds of miles away, so that he can claim her ransom.

As they make their way across the countryside, Arya and the Hound face the challenges of a land beset by war, bandits, pillagers, and enemy soldiers around every corner. The Hound begins to appreciate Arya's determination to seek vengeance on those who have wronged her, and he starts to foster her talents as a killer. Meanwhile, Arya begins to experience sympathy for Sandor Clegane as she learns more about his history and motivations. This presents something of a problem—since the Hound's name is part of Arya's ritual prayer list of those she wants dead.

DAVID BENIOFF AND D. B. WEISS (CO-EXECUTIVE PRODUCERS AND WRITERS): There are no scenes we more enjoyed writing, shooting, and watching than these. Maisie and Rory are operating on a level that begs for a spin-off show. Unfortunately, given how this season ends, this will be difficult. But the biggest testament to their work over this season is the devastating sadness their final scene leaves you with. You wouldn't feel the way you feel at the end of that scene if these characters hadn't found a place in your dark, pitiless heart.

The Hound shows Arya how to be the person she needs to be. Of course, these lessons do change her. They're brutal lessons. But her experience has been brutal as well. For all the horrible things the Hound does, he's not the person who tore Arya's life apart. Well, except the butcher's boy. But you know, sometimes a butcher's boy just has to go.

RORY MCCANN (SANDOR CLEGANE): When the Hound sees Arya acting on her own, there's a feeling that he is watching over her and monitoring her progress. He doesn't seem to mind these side missions of hers, instead offering pointers and asking for advance warning. It's quite amusing in a way—like she's taking a master class in assassination.

BRYAN COGMAN (CO-PRODUCER AND WRITER): Rory's big and tough and intimidating, but what makes his Hound so compelling is that sadness, that weariness in his eyes. Rory has become frighteningly good at the Hound's mood swings—going from vulnerable and almost tender to wild, terrifying, and dangerous. He sort of sneaks up on the viewer as a major character and really comes into his own in seasons three and four.

MAISIE WILLIAMS (ARYA STARK): Toward the end of season three, I think Arya realizes that she has to make a choice about survival. Arya is safer with the Hound than she would be without him, despite the fact she hates him. Later on in season four, I think she starts to understand that her perspective has been quite tunneled, and as she begins to follow the Hound's advice, she becomes quite ruthless herself.

RORY MCCANN (SANDOR CLEGANE): There are echoes, in an odd way, of Arya's relationship with her father, Ned, and his encouragement of her desire to fight. What's interesting is the fact that she has been completely honest about her inclusion of the Hound's name in her prayer, but he continues to look after her. There's definitely something about her honesty and bluntness that he likes, because she manages to get him to talk about the scars his brother gave him. I doubt he's ever opened up before. I doubt he was ever asked.

[OPPOSITE] *The Hound and Arya begin to understand each other.*
[ABOVE] *Arya learns how to fight dirty.*

— BRIENNE VERSUS THE HOUND —

"YOU HEARD THE GIRL. SHE'S NOT COMING WITH YOU."

—THE HOUND

In King's Landing, Brienne of Tarth (Gwendoline Christie) agrees to complete the oath Jaime Lannister once swore to Catelyn Stark: to find and protect her girls, Arya and Sansa. While on the road in Westeros, Brienne unexpectedly crosses paths with Arya and the Hound, Sandor Clegane (Rory McCann). Brienne attempts to convince Arya to leave the Hound and come with her, but Arya is reluctant. Seeing Brienne's Lannister sword, the Hound is immediately distrustful of her true motives. When Brienne declares her intention to take Arya back one way or another, the Hound draws his sword, and a duel between two of the greatest fighters in Westeros begins.

PAUL HERBERT (STUNT COORDINATOR): First, we review the location and use the script beats to map out a general layout for the fight before working out the full choreography. We'll show the actors pictures of the area so they have a mental picture of the terrain. We train the fight in sections, so when we get to the location, if there are any changes, we can rework the order.

The ideal is to use the actors as much as possible—certainly for any close-up work, and then for as much as we can without risking safety. When we bring in the stunt doubles, it is usually for elements that are shot at a distance or in combination with the other actor facing camera. I've found that this can actually help the actors relax because, if they do misjudge a move, the stunt person can make allowances and adjust accordingly. This particular sequence took around three weeks to perfect with the actors in training.

GWENDOLINE CHRISTIE (BRIENNE OF TARTH): The dual was one of the most extraordinary things I have ever experienced. Rory and I are very committed to our characters and portraying them well. We were absolutely focused on executing the sequence. These two well-recognized fighters go up against each other—you know people want to see something magnificent. Rory and I put our hearts in it. That means it feels more personal—you want to experience elements of the fight the way your character would and react like them, too. I don't know how it will be received, but it was certainly one of the best things I've ever done.

RORY MCCANN (SANDOR CLEGANE): I had the most amazing time working with Gwen. That woman has a laugh that rocks planes. She's just great. When we got down to the business of swinging swords at each other, I had to sometimes stop and remind myself that, although we are the same height, I'm a pretty big fellow, and I've been chopping down trees all my life. My god, she's tough, though. Something happens when she puts on her armor. You can see her become a warrior. Suddenly, she had 40 percent more strength and a completely different demeanor.

GWENDOLINE CHRISTIE (BRIENNE OF TARTH): What's great about working with Alex Graves is that he gives you permission to go as far as you want to. There was this moment when Brienne is delivering a volley of punches to the Hound's face,

and she just keeps going until she drives him over the cliff. We'd discussed at length the different ways that we could approach it—would it be silent or vocal, general or personal, mechanical or clinical? In the end, we did three versions of the final push. It actually became quite an upsetting sequence. It became about some of the feelings she might be having in that moment, feelings that I identify with, but she is the one who walks away from it.

RORY MCCANN (SANDOR CLEGANE): Looking back over all the seasons, if I'm honest, this fight scene would be my favorite. I've had other action scenes where knew I was in a "moment," but they were just so uncomfortable to film, be it the heat in the cave or some other element. To be in the environment in Iceland and in that unbelievably special location—I really just wanted to stay.

[OPPOSITE] *Despite her victory, Brienne realizes that she's lost her prize, Arya.*
[ABOVE] *Two gladiators battle for supremacy.*

Part Seven

BECOMING A QUEEN

"I will do what queens do. I will rule."

— Daenerys Targaryen

Under the desert sun in Essos, Daenerys Targaryen continues to make her way toward her ultimate goal, the Iron Throne. But first, she is determined to build an army by conquering the three main cities on Slaver's Bay: Astapor, Yunkai, and Meereen. At Astapor, Dany defeats the Good Masters and brings the Unsullied warriors under her command. At Yunkai, Dany gathers the support of the Second Sons and their new leader, Daario Naharis, and with them, she successfully overthrows the Wise Masters and incites a slave revolt. Now Daenerys faces her greatest challenge yet, to battle the Great Masters for control of the legendary and sprawling city of Meereen to the north.

SLAVER'S BAY:
A BRIEF HISTORY

DORY JIM KOTAS TEBAGHO JIVA DERVE, SOMBAZI. LU JI EBAT, JIMI SYDLIVAS ZER MAZMAGHO.
["NO ONE CAN GIVE YOU YOUR FREEDOM, BROTHER. IF YOU WANT IT, YOU MUST TAKE IT."]

—GREY WORM

AROUND FIVE THOUSAND YEARS before the war known as Robert's Rebellion, the ancient city of Ghis was the capital of the sprawling and powerful Ghiscari Empire on the continent of Essos. Founded by Grazdan the Great, the rich lands were protected by a seemingly undefeatable legion with a fearsome reputation. Then, over a succession of wars, the Valyrian Freehold and its all-powerful dragons laid waste to the Ghiscari Empire. Ghis, on the shores of the Gulf of Grief, was reduced to rubble, the buildings burnt to cinders by the dragons and the once-fertile fields sown with salt, sulfur, and skulls.

After the fall of Valyria, the scattered remains of the Ghiscari people rebuilt the three great cities of Slaver's Bay: Yunkai, Astapor, and Meereen. Fulfilling its name, the region still depends on the riches brought in by the massive slave trade, which is overseen by masters in each city. Little of the great civilization of Ghiscari has survived into the present, yet one element remains: the sigil of the harpy. This fantastical creature with a woman's torso, clawed wings, the legs of an eagle, and a twisted scorpion tail appears in all the cities of Slaver's Bay, a symbolic reminder of the region's glorious past.

[PREVIOUS SPREAD] *Danaerys surveys a freshly conquered Slaver's Bay.*
[ABOVE] *A map of Slaver's Bay.* [OPPOSITE] *The Great Pyramid in Meereen towers over the city, a slaver's harpy perched on top.*

— CREATING MEEREEN —

"EVERY CITY YOU'VE CONQUERED COULD SIT WITHIN HER WALLS, AND STILL LEAVE ROOM FOR MORE. THEY SAY A THOUSAND SLAVES DIED BUILDING THE GREAT PYRAMID OF MEEREEN."

—MISSANDEI

For Daenerys, the most formidable obstacle to conquering Slaver's Bay is the massive city of Meereen, whose walls could hold the people of Yunkai and Astapor combined. Rising high above the city is the Great Pyramid, built by slaves centuries before. Also of note is the Temple of Graces. One of many temples that fill the city, its singular size and great golden dome form yet another symbol of the city's wealth.

After Daenerys successfully wins the city and crucifies the Great Masters, she takes up residence in the penthouse at the top of the Great Pyramid. Claiming her first throne, she holds court in the audience chamber, beginning her transition to becoming a ruler.

When it came to creating the city of Meereen itself, the greatest challenge for the art department was the scale of the interior sets. Designing Meereen was one of the first tasks for the new production designer, Deb Riley, who took over from Gemma Jackson when she left the show at the end of season three.

GEORGE R. R. MARTIN (CO-EXECUTIVE PRODUCER AND AUTHOR): When it comes to influences, I avoid looking at a single historical reference or person to create something like Slaver's Bay. There are certainly elements from the Babylonian and Mesopotamian societies of ancient times. There are Carthaginian and ancient Persian factors. And of course, there is a good deal of purely imaginative creation. The trick is to blend them all together to construct a world that is entirely your own.

DEB RILEY (PRODUCTION DESIGNER): I felt very lucky to walk into the world that Gemma Jackson had created. It gave me a lot of confidence. When it came to the new worlds, it was a case of establishing contrasts. If King's Landing was increasingly about opulence, Meereen was about monolithic structures and austere but intimidating impressions through exotic and rich designs. It was wonderful to be able to work on a world that had not been seen before.

BRYAN COGMAN (CO-PRODUCER AND WRITER): Deb Riley's designs for Meereen in particular really stand out as wildly different from anything we'd seen on the show. Dany's audience chamber in the Great Pyramid is so grand and beautifully textured—audiences will absolutely think it's some palace we found in Croatia, but no. It's a soundstage in Belfast!

DEB RILEY (PRODUCTION DESIGNER): The wonderful thing about the audience hall was being able to build a heavy set. The plasterers took such pride in their elements; you walk into that room, and there is a resonance and headiness to it. It almost seems to hum when you step in. David and Dan were very keen to be clear that it was within a pyramid, which allowed us to bring in the slanted ceiling. Clearly, the pyramid was far bigger, which is why only one wall is on an angle and why in Dany's penthouse there is the pinnacle shape.

TOM MARTIN (CONSTRUCTION MANAGER): The audience hall was a huge set with a thirty-six-foot-high ceiling.

The walls themselves were clad in many types of different relief panels, each one handmade with individual textures and paint finishes to indicate the different stages of aging. Surrounding the main staircase we built in a low-level pool to catch the light and reflect the carved motifs on the sides of the stairs. The detailing in the room is immense; on the floor there are hundreds of individually modeled tiles, each hand-painted. Behind the throne, the wall is covered in tiny mosaic tiles that have been highlighted with gold and bronze, numbering in the thousands.

DEB RILEY (PRODUCTION DESIGNER): Usually, when there is the presence of a pyramid, the mind goes to Egypt. What was wonderful about this season was being able to bring in more in terms of texture, and Meereen was the perfect opportunity to do it. When you look at the architecture of the Mayans and the step pyramids, you see a tremendous amount of sculpture and iconography that has softened but remains beautiful. As a slave city, Meereen could have created these buildings on a huge scale. It was interesting to imagine the sort of skilled artisan that would have been available to create these newly textured elements.

TOM MARTIN (CONSTRUCTION MANAGER): In terms of the crew, the penthouse seemed to be one of the most popular sets of the series. I think that has to do with the finishes being so tactile and beautiful. Imagining the heat of the desert, Deb and her team designed intricate air vents that would allow the building to cool, each appearing to be carved out of the stonework. Pivotal to the design of the space was the inclusion of the revolving wooden screens that could be opened to create different areas. Sandwiched between each of the frames was real silk, creating a staggering effect when light was diffused through the fabric. The ceiling was finished with reclaimed timber panels radiating out from the center and supported by massive timber beams, while the floor was made up of huge handmade and hand-painted flagstones, each one distressed to reflect the age of the building.

NATHALIE EMMANUEL (MISSANDEI): We walk into these complete sets, dressed in these beautiful costumes, and when you look at the work, the hundreds of tiny elements, you can't help but be in the moment. Our senses are already absorbing everything we are surrounded by, and it makes it seem almost natural to be standing in this world.

[ABOVE] *The penthouse realized.* [OPPOSITE] *Daenerys has a difficult decision to make.* [FOLLOWING SPREAD] *Daenerys claims her first real throne in Meereen.*

DAARIO NAHARIS

"I ONLY HAVE TWO TALENTS IN THIS WORLD: WAR AND WOMEN."

—DAARIO NAHARIS

Born the bastard son of a whore, Daario Naharis (Michiel Huisman) grew into an exceptional and fearless fighter, rising to become a lieutenant for the mercenary Second Sons. Daario first meets Daenerys outside the walls of Yunkai while accompanying Captains Mero and Prendahl na Ghezn as they consider Daenerys's offer: to fight for her and abandon their contract to defend Yunkai for the Wise Masters. Later, the captains, certain of victory, decide to assassinate Daenerys, but Daario is too enchanted by Daenerys's beauty to allow this. Instead, he kills the captains and returns to Daenerys, presenting her with the captains' heads as a mark of his loyalty and with the army of the Second Sons to help her conquer Yunkai.

At Meereen, Daario offers himself for one-on-one combat with the Meereen champion. When he defeats the champion in spectacular fashion, Daario delivers the allegiance of the city's slaves, which leads to a revolt that allows Daenerys to capture Meereen. Despite the reservations of her advisors, Daenerys finds herself drawn to the new leader of the Second Sons, and they soon become lovers.

MICHIEL HUISMAN (DAARIO NAHARIS): It's a dream role. Playing a character who is so tough, but with a little bit of fun—and a little bit of swagger. He's a self-made man. He wasn't born into a knighthood. He isn't a royal. He's built himself up from nothing—these are great characteristics to play around with. He's very self-assured and unapologetic about it. I think it adds to his appeal.

EMILIA CLARKE (DAENERYS TARGARYEN): In my mind, Dany will never love anyone the way she loved Khal Drogo, but she is becoming a different person. Taking control of her newfound womanhood comes with its own wants and desires. I think she's testing out her confidence on Daario; in a way, he's a bit of a plaything. Above all, she's learning to be a leader, a commander, a queen, and then a woman—in that order. She is always thinking with multiple roles in mind. While she enjoys Daario, he is ultimately one of her soldiers. She needs to be able to put him in the most strategic position for her needs. She's also a woman, and she doesn't have the freedom a male ruler would to sow his seed. She knows she can't be invested in anything other than her babies [the dragons] and her mission, especially with someone who doesn't care about the rules at all.

MICHIEL HUISMAN (DAARIO NAHARIS): When it comes to his relationship with Dany, it's clear he's attracted by her beauty, but he lives for two things: the fight and women. He sees her as the ultimate woman because she has beauty and this underlying strength. She also has a vulnerability—she really cares for the people—and he recognizes that he doesn't really have that himself. He sees that, by being close to her, he can grow. While he is aware of Jorah's feelings and respects him, he ultimately wants to be with Dany, so that's what he's going to do. This creates a conflict that doesn't happen with Grey Worm—I think Daario is trying to push Grey Worm the way an older brother would, to try and bring him out from his shell.

GREY WORM

"'GREY WORM' GIVES ME PRIDE. IT IS A LUCKY NAME. THE NAME THIS ONE WAS BORN WITH WAS CURSED. THAT WAS THE NAME HE HAD WHEN HE WAS TAKEN AS A SLAVE. BUT GREY WORM IS THE NAME THIS ONE HAD THE DAY DAENERYS STORMBORN SET HIM FREE."

—GREY WORM

Grey Worm (Jacob Anderson) is the democratically elected captain of the Unsullied army. He was chosen for this role after the defeat of the Good Masters in Astapor. He has no recollection of family or of life before becoming an Unsullied soldier, which is likely due to the young age at which he was taken into training. Fiercely loyal to Daenerys and her cause to free all slaves, Grey Worm has proven himself to be a strong military strategist and a valuable asset to Daenerys in her campaigns. He is learning to trust his instincts as he gains confidence in himself. Initially only able to speak Low Valyrian, Grey Worm has begun to learn the common tongue under Missandei's patient guidance.

JACOB ANDERSON (GREY WORM): Initially, I was confused about how much of his humanity could come out. Dan said something incredibly useful early on—that I should think of Grey Worm as walking trauma. I think of him as human somewhere in that, but with layers so thick that it's hard to see. I wanted to have tiny moments where you can see it. That's been the hardest thing, working with the directors and David and Dan to figure out when that can happen and how much can come out. He's never been anything. He's never been anyone. Then suddenly this angel appears and says, "Be something different, if you choose to." The idea of choice is completely alien.

EMILIA CLARKE (DAENERYS TARGARYEN): By asking the Unsullied to vote for their leader, Dany gained an immediate sense of trust in Grey Worm's abilities. I think she looked him in the eye and saw his integrity. She saw someone that she could, perhaps not trust, but rely on to act on her orders when required and be merciful when needed.

[OPPOSITE] *Daario takes on the champion of Meereen.*
[ABOVE] *Jacob Anderson portrays the captain of the Unsullied.*

MISSANDEI

PINDAS SKO JI YN TEBILA, VA ME RUDHY. PINDAS SKO GOMILA KIZI SIR.
["SHE ASKS THAT YOU GIVE ME TO HER, AS A PRESENT. SHE ASKS THAT YOU DO THIS NOW."]

—MISSANDEI

Missandei (Nathalie Emmanuel) was a slave in the service of the Good Master known as Kraznys mo Nakloz when she caught Daenerys's attention in the slave markets of Astapor. Taken from her home in Naath when she was very young, Missandei remembers little of her life before servitude, but she has managed to become a gifted translator with knowledge of nineteen languages. Given to Daenerys at the young khaleesi's request, Missandei becomes as close to a confidante and friend as Daenerys will allow.

NATHALIE EMMANUEL (MISSANDEI): As season four goes on, we are getting to see more of Missandei as a person, rather than a thing or a slave. She's becoming a human with feelings and you see more of her depth of character and her talent. The way she has been written makes you feel deeply for her; it's so sweet and sad. Being able to play with that as an actress is very exciting, to be able to see her as her own person rather than speaking only other people's words. The fact that Dany asks her things makes her words important. I think Daenerys is her first friend; she's being allowed to be who she is. On the other hand, growing up a slave means she will always be quite self-contained. She's been conditioned to be that way, and she's slow to trust.

EMILIA CLARKE (DAENERYS TARGARYEN): There is a complication between men and women that doesn't exist here. Dany has never had any sort of maternal influence, anything nurturing ever. There is something about the relationship between Missandei and Dany that can only ever happen between two women. Dany wants to trust her; she even asks her to always be there when she says, "Don't betray me." Her journey really began with the desire to save a woman being violated; she saw herself within that situation. In some ways Missandei is her constant reminder that there will always be another woman. There is always more good to do in the world.

NATHALIE EMMANUEL (MISSANDEI): We don't really know a huge amount about Missandei's history, but you can assume that she would have been used for other things than translations by men—beaten and abused. She definitely has a mistrust of men, so a straightforward relationship with a woman where that isn't an issue is completely new to her.

BARRISTAN SELMY

"I'VE BEEN SEARCHING FOR YOU, DAENERYS STORMBORN. TO BEG YOUR FORGIVENESS. I WAS SWORN TO PROTECT YOUR FAMILY. I FAILED THEM. I AM BARRISTAN SELMY, KINGSGUARD TO YOUR FATHER. ALLOW ME TO JOIN YOUR QUEENSGUARD, AND I WILL NOT FAIL YOU AGAIN."

—BARRISTAN SELMY

Barristan Selmy (Ian McElhinney) remains one of the greatest living knights in Westerosi history. He served as a member of the Kingsguard for Aerys Targaryen, and he remained loyal to House Targaryen throughout Robert's Rebellion. However, because of the tremendous respect Ser Barristan had earned through his service, he was pardoned when Robert Baratheon come to power. Ser Barristan served Robert faithfully as Lord Commander of the Kingsguard, and after Robert's death, he retained his position under King Joffrey. That is, until Joffrey declared Barristan unfit for service due to old age. Mocked by the court, disgusted by the behavior of Cersei and Joffrey, and insulted that Jaime Lannister would replace him, Barristan traveled to Astapor in search of Daenerys Targaryen (Emilia Clarke), his new queen. After saving Daenerys from a manticore—part of an assassination attempt by the Warlocks of Qarth—Ser Barristan pledges to serve her in her Queensguard.

IAN MCELHINNEY (BARRISTAN SELMY): You could definitely argue that Barristan is one of the true honorable characters, one of the only "good" men in the piece. There are some who would argue he switched sides, but it was with a royal pardon. In my mind, I've always thought of him—and I think the audience does, too—as loyal and decent, "the honorable man." Now that he is in Daenerys's court, he will do anything to prove his loyalty and, in his mind, hopefully serve someone who is a good ruler.

[OPPOSITE] *Nathalie Emmanuel portrays Missandei, bandmaiden to Daenerys.*
[ABOVE] *Ian McElhinney portrays new advisor Barristan Selmy.*

— BANISHING JORAH —
EPISODE 408: "THE MOUNTAIN AND THE VIPER"

"YOU SOLD MY SECRETS TO THE MAN WHO KILLED MY FATHER AND STOLE MY BROTHER'S THRONE. YOU WANT ME TO FORGIVE YOU?"

—DAENERYS TARGARYEN

Throughout her time in exile—ever since her marriage to Khal Drogo, when she became the khaleesi *of Drogo's* khalasar*— Daenerys Targaryen has placed her trust in Jorah Mormont (Iain Glen), who has been her most steadfast and loyal advisor. Jorah educated her about local customs, advised her on military strategy, and fought by her side through a myriad of challenges. In a market outside Vaes Dothrak: Jorah recognized and stopped an assassination attempt on the young queen, proving to Daenerys his loyalty and concern for her safety.*

Then Daenerys discovers the truth: Barristan has discovered that the exiled knight provided information on her to King's Landing, and in exchange he received a pardon. This revelation brings Dany's trust in Jorah to an end. Jorah protests that he renounced this betrayal long ago, but Dany banishes him from her dominion forever. This act leaves Daenerys a changed woman, and it returns Jorah to his former life, as a disgraced wanderer in exile.

EMILIA CLARKE (DAENERYS TARGARYEN): It's interesting to me that Dany can be merciful with the outside world, but those closest to her are burdened with a far more exacting standard. In many ways, I feel like the core of who Daenerys has become is related to the loss of her husband and the loss of her child. In that moment, to discover what she does about Jorah—I believe that she places every scrap of blame at his feet. She feels that he put them in the crosshairs, that his action led to the assassination attempt of the wine seller and all the dominoes that fell from there.

BRYAN COGMAN (CO-PRODUCER AND WRITER): I think viewers take for granted, much as Dany does, that Jorah will always be there—giving sage advice, support, and protection to the *khaleesi*. So when he's dismissed so abruptly, in shame and disgrace, it's a real blow to the characters and viewer. Emilia and Iain are amazing in that scene, so much so that director Alex Graves kept the entire thing tight on their faces—very few cutaways or establishing shots. It's very powerful.

EMILIA CLARKE (DAENERYS TARGARYEN): It's the worst possible time to be dealt such a blow. There's a moment in that scene—she's felt the betrayal so deeply that you can almost see the flip of the coin between madness and genius in her. There's no question that she chooses exile [for Jorah] knowing that that type of purgatory is the worst possible punishment for him, more so even than death.

[RIGHT] *Jorah Mormont, one of the key advisors to Daenerys during her campaigns until his earlier treachery is discovered.* [FOLLOWING SPREADS] *In season three, multiple layers show the VFX process that brings the dragons to life; Daenerys's greatest weapon is the threat of what her dragons will become.*

— CREATING THE DRAGONS —

"THEY ARE DRAGONS, *KHALEESI*. THEY CAN NEVER BE TAMED. NOT EVEN BY THEIR MOTHER."

—JORAH MORMONT

Of course, Dany's three young dragons—Drogon, Rhaegal, and Viserion—represent a potentially dominant and perhaps unstoppable military force, but for many they also represent something more: they are apparitions from a time forgotten, a time of legends. For the VFX team, the constant task is to create creatures that are both fantastical and yet grounded in reality. This challenge has only grown along with the dragons, as they increase in size and ability.

JOE BAUER (VFX SUPERVISOR): In terms of reference, the design of the dragons is based on the movements and shape of bats and eagles. Of course, as they are carrying more size and weight, they are also displacing more air to hold them aloft. When it comes to performance, each one is developing a different personality—one is cunning, another more aggressive, and of course, Drogon is the alpha, the lion of the pride. They are supposed to be increasingly wild, dangerous, and unpredictable.

STEVE KULLBACK (VFX PRODUCER): The dragons are designed under Joe's supervision by Dan Katcher, who begins the initial sculpting using z-brush, before moving over to Maya for the modeling, texture, and lighting. For us, though, it's less about what program we create in and more about the way it's created. We have an incredibly gifted team that work from Pixomondo in Frankfurt. The dimension and scale have become much more prevalent; it's less about the size and detail of the head and more about the body length and wingspan—which is about twenty-eight feet on Drogon, who is approximately 15 percent larger than the other two. A huge amount of work goes into creating the details that suggest a physical threat, taking inspiration from real elements in nature to insure the dragons look as realistic as possible.

JOE BAUER (VFX SUPERVISOR): Aside from bats and eagles, we also look at reptilian examples—monitor lizards and komodo dragons—for particular looks. In terms of attitude, we consider Drogon to have a personality of a lion, and Rhaegal and Viserion to be great white sharks. There's a sort of nobility, but also a viciousness. When it comes to their specific weight, we haven't actually worked it out. Instead, we have focused on what scale works best visually.

STEVE KULLBACK (VFX PRODUCER): We also don't know how many teeth they have—just that they do, and that they look gnarly.

JOE BAUER (VFX SUPERVISOR): Also, they push out their teeth during attacks. We took that and the eye roll from the great white. There is something about the fact that we have all absorbed a little from things we have seen, nature shows and such, that helps lend the dragons more realism.

DAVID BENIOFF AND D. B. WEISS (CO-EXECUTIVE PRODUCERS AND WRITERS): A while ago, we asked the VFX team to draw up a dragon growth chart, tracking them season by season to get them where we needed them by season seven or so. They eat a lot in the off-season, apparently. We love them and pay extra attention to them, especially at the beginning of each season when the final looks are being set—but the credit here belongs to Joe, Steve, Adam, and all the guys at Pixomondo. God is in the details with Dany's babies, and every breath, blink, stretch, and snort has been so lovingly worked over.

In the beginning, we were worried that we wouldn't get the execution right. But assuming that they were done well—and we think the guys have gone above and beyond on that score—we were never afraid of them as an element of the show. They were crucial to the show from its conception.

EMILIA CLARKE (DAENERYS TARGARYEN): It is a challenge to react to something that isn't there, but for me, from day one, the idea of the dragons and what they represent is so strong, it almost makes sense that they would be imagined. It's always amazing to see what my mind has manifested made real. The first time I saw them, I was really ill. I was lying prone in bed, and my brother was watching in another room. I actually heard them first, and my reaction was visceral. I ran to the other room thinking, "My babies!" It's quite incredible to see them brought to life.

PART EIGHT

A DIFFERENT WAR

"*Those are giants down there! Riding mammoths! You think your cold-rolled steel is going to stop them?*"

—JON SNOW

WHILE THE GREAT HOUSES OF WESTEROS CONTINUE FIGHTING ONE ANOTHER FOR THE IRON THRONE, DIFFERENT CONCERNS ANIMATE THE PLAYERS NORTH OF THE WALL. BRAN STARK AND HIS COMPANIONS ARE BATTLING FOR SURVIVAL, AGAINST ALL ODDS, IN ORDER TO FOLLOW THE STRANGE VISIONS GUIDING THEM TOWARD A LIFE-CHANGING DESTINY. MEANWHILE, JON SNOW AND THE NIGHT'S WATCH FACE AN INVADING WILDLING ARMY UNLIKE ANY SEEN BEFORE, EITHER IN SIZE OR COMPOSITION. SOMEHOW, THOUGH THEY HAVE LOST THEIR LEADER COMMANDER MORMONT, AND THEIR FORCES ARE DEPLETED AND STILL REELING FROM THE REVOLT AT CRASTER'S KEEP, THE MEN OF THE NIGHT'S WATCH MUST STRUGGLE TO DEFEND THE WALL AND UPHOLD THEIR OATHS TO PROTECT ALL OF WESTEROS FROM THE TERRORS THAT HAVE COME KNOCKING AT THEIR DOOR.

— BUILDING THE IRON BANK —

"You can't run from them, you can't cheat them, you can't sway them with excuses. If you owe them money and you don't want to crumble yourself, you pay it back."

—Tywin Lannister

Stannis Baratheon is driven by an unrele[...]
the Iron Throne from the Lannisters. With [...]
the powers Melisandre seems to hold after t[...]
Stannis agrees to follow his vision of a grea[...]
responds to the call for assistance from the [...]

the Battle of Blackwater Bay. Then
[...]eaworth suggests a new alliance, this
[...]k of Braavos—the first glimpse of a

DEB RILEY (PRODUCTION DESIG[...]
very first creative meetings that I had in LA[...]
with Dan Weiss about the work of Albert [...]
ture of the Nazis—about how architecture[...]
idate. That was precisely the tone they w[...]
verticality and strength of the designs. It [...]
Iron Bank, which is one of the richest inst[...]
loved the idea that there is one table, and [...]
on that table. Applying the *Game of Thrones*[...]
with such a strong perspective was very e[...]
insane things about the set was that it wa[...]

[...]ION DESIGNER): Nothing says
[...]ed marble floor. Something Gemma
[...]olor pallets for each new environment,
[...]hat here. The richness of that green
[...]s. The finish was so beautiful you would
[...]l painted marble. It was a nightmare
[...]g days, everyone had to wear little boo-
[...]was worth it to have these marvellous
[...]that in King's Landing. When you walk
[...]ating, just because of the sound it cre-
[...] successful.

TOM MARTIN (CONSTRUCTION[...]
the course of an eight-week build, the t[...]
sides of the bank, which were filled in l[...]
the design allowed us to use twenty-foo[...]
one full side of the chamber. Each of the door panels [...]
twelve feet high; they were modeled gold panels inset into the
bronze frame. Each section was designed to depict the investment
interests of the bank; for example, shipbuilding or scenes of
warfare. The floor, a high-polished dark green marble, was made
up of seven hundred individually marbled and dip-dyed tiles, so
there were no repeats in the stone.

[...]-PRODUCER AND WRITER): I
[...]he clean lines, the shiny marble floor,
[...]nidates anyone who dares enter in seek
[...]scene to shoot—what other fantasy
[...]ial side of things?

[PREVIOUS SPREAD] *Jon Snow enters the wildling camp, with one mission in mind—to end the assault on the Wall, even if it costs him his life.* [OPPOSITE (TOP)] *Stannis and Davos meet with the Bank.* [OPPOSITE (BOTTOM)] *Between set-ups, the set floor was polished for every mark.* [ABOVE] *Concept art of the Iron Bank.*

— CREATING THE MAMMOTHS AND GIANTS —

Game of Thrones *has staged many epic action sequences, but the Battle for the Wall in Episode 409, "The Watchers on the Wall," was arguably the largest battle ever. Key to the spectacle was the appearance of mammoths and giants within the wildling army. As the Giants used their massive strength to fire arrows to the top of the towering wall, the Mammoths were used to pull apart the gates at the foundations, a force unseen before and seemingly* unstoppable *due to their massive and dominating size. In this episode, the mammoths were created by the VFX team, and the giants were conjured by the prosthetics and the costume teams. The VFX department also oversaw a good deal of the giants' green screen and on-set work and ensured that their interactions with the mammoths were to scale and believable.*

STEVE KULLBACK (VFX PRODUCER): The mammoth was approximately twenty-two feet tall from ground to head, fifteen feet wide, and eighteen feet long. When it comes time to shoot, the mammoth needs to live in a space that actors are performing in, so we needed a stuffie similar to what we used with the direwolves. You need to be able to frame up your shots, and the actors need to know what to leave space for, how to react appropriately. Joe Bauer came up with the idea of using a space frame and he worked together with Stuart [Brisdon, VFX] to design a lightweight steel frame that could be carried around by four people as a placeholder. A second frame was made for the shots with the giants that was half the size, which allows the scale to be proportionally accurate.

JOE BAUER (VFX SUPERVISOR): At one point there was some consideration of using elephants dressed in special mammoth suits. It's actually been done before in the movie *Quest for Fire*. We considered it because it seemed like a CG mammoth that would look right and be effective would be out of our budget, and this might be our best secondary option. Animal behavior and all that hair? It's just about the most expensive CG thing you can ask for. We got incredibly lucky. The vendor MPC made available to us models they had started for other reasons, which were within our budget.

JOE BAUER (VFX SUPERVISOR): The giants were first developed in season three. The best decision was to use unusually tall performers to give a sense of a great deal of weight to the giants' movement. Ian Whyte measures in at around seven feet, one inch in height. He is a well-known suit performer in the UK, and he had been our giant before, as well as a White Walker in season one. Production then found Neil Fingleton, the tallest man in the UK, who in his suit comes in around seven feet, eleven inches. We also slowed down the speed on-screen a tiny amount. In terms of design, the idea was that we would always be looking up at them, so the costumes were deliberately made smaller at the top with big tree trunk legs at the bottom.

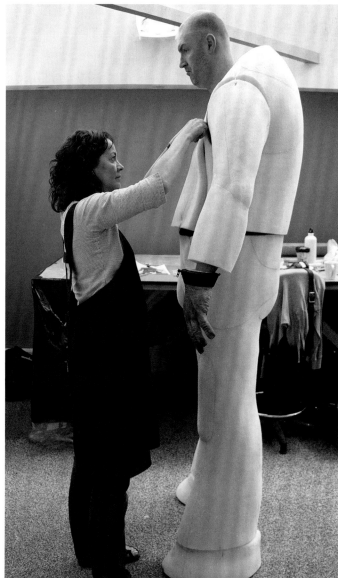

BARRIE GOWER (PROSTHETICS SUPERVISOR): We had two giants, Mag the Mighty and Dongo the Doomed. We inherited the molds from season three, but we wanted to rework some of the detailing and the hair. It begins with foam body suits that create the overall shape of the giant, but they are brought to life by the amazing animal-skin costumes and raw finished weapons.

To get the suit, we begin by making a full-body cast. Then a fabricator created the suit by layering and piecing reticulated foam into a creation that could actually be zipped up. For Neil Fingleton's suit, we sewed in a set of his own shoes for comfort. The costume team then dressed the foam suit, but we still needed to create a new silicon prosthetic headpiece for the second giant, which was designed from scratch. The head alone was several kilos, so they are carrying a great deal of weight when they move—I think this might help with the lumbering. Prosthetics alone takes three hours of application for the heads. We were eventually able to get down to around one-and-a-half hours, so with hair and costume the process could take between three and five hours for each of our giants.

NEIL MARSHALL (DIRECTOR): Bringing in the mammoths and giants adds a whole new dimension to what's happening north of the Wall, creating a real spectacle in the way that the arrival of tanks and planes might. The wildlings use the mammoths in a very strategic way, trying to use their strength to breach the gate. Logistically, this meant that the army north of the Wall becomes quite CGI heavy. Because of the need for different image references, some things needed to be shot three times over. It reminded me of the scene in *The Empire Strikes Back* when the Imperial AT-AT Walkers appear from the snow. They lend a weight, a gravitas, to the assault.

[OPPOSITE] *The giants dominate in battle.* [ABOVE (LEFT)] *Green screen filming captures the mammoth riders.* [ABOVE (RIGHT)] *Starting to build the bodies of the giants during the test stages.*

— THE BATTLE FOR THE WALL —
EPISODE 409: "THE WATCHERS ON THE WALL"

"BROTHERS! A HUNDRED GENERATIONS HAVE DEFENDED THIS CASTLE! SHE HAS NEVER FALLEN BEFORE. SHE WILL NOT FALL TONIGHT!"

—SER ALLISER THORNE

Time has run out for the Night's Watch. The wildlings have arrived at the Wall, determined to breach the gates and invade Westeros. Their army includes giants, mammoths, and the cannibilistic Thenn, who hunger for more than blood. All are ready to conquer the Wall and the depleted Night's Watch forces trying valiantly to prevent their success. For Jon Snow and Samwell Tarly, life will be changed forever by the loss of friends and the security of the Wall. Jon must assume the mantle of leader and with it the burden of sacrifice for the greater good above personal preference. For Sam, it is a chance to assert himself as a man of knowledge and experience, to prove that his place in the Watch has been earned and to work with Jon as an equal to play his part in the battle.

The "Battle for the Wall" in Episode 409 was the most ambitious scene in the series to date, and director Neil Marshall

returned to lead the charge. Filmed on three separate sets and with one being the largest set built to date, the action took place on every possible level.

While one whole cell of the Paint Hall was filled completely by the set for the top of the Wall, two more sets were to be found in the depths of Magheramorne quarry—Castle Black and the base of the Wall.

At night the base of the Wall was besieged by CGI mammoths and prosthetic giants, while the courtyard of Castle Black, perched high above, echoed with the sounds of battle as hundreds of extras, stuntmen, and cast fought for survival and the future of Westeros.

[OPPOSITE] *Jon Snow takes on Styr in the courtyard of Castle Black.*
[ABOVE] *Sam and Gilly find themselves thrown in the path of danger once again.*

NEIL MARSHALL (DIRECTOR): There was no way around the need for the set of the top of the Wall. We simply couldn't achieve what we needed in some hole dug out of the ground. It needed to be all snow and ice, so it made sense to be built from scratch. We deliberately created something that was going to be horrible to fight in. We ended up with a huge set twenty-five feet off the ground. So if you weren't about to fall off the edge, you were crushed into these tight trenches. Logistically, it was a nightmare to film on because the space is so tight. We didn't make it easy for ourselves, but the effect looks amazing.

DEB RILEY (PRODUCTION DESIGNER): With the top of the Wall, the art department reference was the Somme. It's something people are familiar with when they think of the horrors of war, so there's a sort of instant recognition. It was interesting and humbling to see the way the men fought in the trenches and then made it their own—then play with how that might be done in the snow. I was also fascinated by the scale—the Wall is over seven hundred feet high, but how wide is it? What direction do certain things face? I also wanted to include the nonlinear lines of the zig-zag trenches, giving you an opportunity to be surprised by what's around the corner.

TOM MARTIN (CONSTRUCTION MANAGER): This was by far one of the most challenging sets to complete. The set itself took up most of the space in the stage, built on top of a fourteen-foot steel frame that towered above the floor. Sculpted out of over four hundred blocks of fireproof polystyrene, it took twelve modelers six weeks to complete. Once the set was finished and plastered, over five tons of hot wax were sprayed on the walls, creating the same ice effect as in season three. To make the set look as real as possible, we used reclaimed timber to act as the supports in the trenches.

The size of the set also required one of the largest hand-painted scenic backing ever created in Europe—measuring sixty-five-feet high and over-three-hundred-feet long.

NEIL MARSHALL (DIRECTOR): Moving to the exterior location meant there was more scope for SFX. I like to be the person who pushes the boundaries of what can be achieved on a set. I wanted the scale of the stunts with the fire at the base of the Wall to be big. Ultimately, these guys are getting barrels of boiling oil dropped on them and that would be pretty nasty. We had amazing stuntmen who were able to be in the middle of an actual explosion and engulfed in flames. We only did it twice, but that was all that was needed.

STUART BRISDON (SFX SUPERVISOR): The explosion of the burning oil onto the mammoth was something that I worked on personally. After seemingly endless tests over two weeks, what we came up with was propelling the fuel forward and up from three separate points to create a wall of fire. Each point held within it three "mortar" pots holding 1.5 liters of fuel and a separate charge (nine all together). In addition we had three buried lots of a thickened fuel slurry, so that after it began to fall, you would have the flames falling through the air and littering the ground. This season we have reached new levels with the action sequences.

NEIL MARSHALL (DIRECTOR): From the beginning this was a much more complex proposition. "Blackwater" [Episode 209] was really one army getting in ships, landing on the beaches, and running for the gate—it was quite linear. The battle for the Wall is on two fronts: you have characters south of the Wall fighting a battle, an army to the north, and stuck in between are the defending forces. It's really three separate groups to keep connected, but the distances are so vast. For instance, the Wall is supposed to be over seven hundred feet high, so no bow could reach the top—it keeps that group quite isolated. No one would be at risk. By giving the giants bows, it's like bringing in the heavy artillery. They bring everything together. I have it so that a giant fires his bow, and the arrow is so powerful that it picks a guy up from the top of the Wall and deposits him in the courtyard of Castle Black in the middle of the fight there.

KIT HARINGTON (JON SNOW): To talk about the battle means to talk about how amazing the stuntmen on the show really are. The set pieces they come up with are remarkable. [Sword master] C. C. Smiff is so patient and enthusiastic. He knows there is no point in having a scene where the background actors are running around like headless chickens. He gives a huge amount of attention to the crowd performers. That's as it should be in my mind—we are an ensemble.

NEIL MARSHALL (DIRECTOR): Kit had just come off a feature where he had spent months training in fighting techniques and was in peak physical condition. He's got such a natural fluid ability, anyway; he's like a young Errol Flynn. In terms of his character, I felt like we had spent three years building up Jon as a great fighter, so it had to be good. It was amazing being able to cut any restraints and see what he's truly capable of.

DAVID BENIOFF AND D. B. WEISS (CO-EXECUTIVE PRODUCERS AND WRITERS): We give Neil Marshall a limited budget and production schedule, and he somehow crafts a full-on cinematic experience. And he gets wonderful, emotional performances on top of it. The 360 shot. The Giant's arrow carrying a hapless Night's Watchman off the top of the Wall and into the courtyard. The dropping of the Scythe. The mammoth pulling the gates. Mag the Mighty charging through the tunnel. The shot of Jon Snow holding Ygritte in his arms. This may not be an action shot, but it may be our favorite shot of the entire season.

NEIL MARSHALL (DIRECTOR): The 360 shot was something I wanted from the moment that I set foot in the Castle Black courtyard. To have something that is all-encompassing is much more visually interesting. I decided that the action would be choreographed around the edges, with some fighting in the middle. Similar to the giant's arrow, I used the shot to track the positions of the main characters within the battle. Up until this point, we had seen them all individually, so essentially this tied them together geographically. We were incredibly fortunate. On the night of the shoot, we spent an hour rehearsing before getting it in seven takes.

BRYAN COGMAN (CO-PRODUCER AND WRITER): The ninth episode of season four is arguably our most action-packed episode yet, but it's an emotional sucker punch as well with the death of Ygritte. From a story standpoint, I love it because it finally delivers on something we've been slowly teasing since the first episode: Jon Snow as hero. He really comes into his own. And it's a major hour for Samwell Tarly, too, with John Bradley giving a knockout performance as Sam. But, in the end, this episode is a testament to our incredible, dedicated, tireless crew, who are the best in the business, period.

JOHN BRADLEY (SAMWELL TARLY): Sam's journey with Gilly back to the Wall and escaping the White Walkers has put him in a real position of power with certain members of the Night's Watch because he's got all this knowledge. It's as if he's discovered his value, and it's quite a unique value at that. Fighting is something that any number of people can do relatively well, but the academic elements are not.

KIT HARINGTON (JON SNOW): Jon's never had much to lose, but by this battle he's basically got nothing. He knows what he has to do to protect the people south of the Wall, and he starts to recognize that his love of the men and his ability to lead could allow him to follow on from Commander Mormont, even if it is out of necessity rather than desire.

JOHN BRADLEY (SAMWELL TARLY): When Sam first arrived, you couldn't imagine him protecting anyone, but he's taken care of Gilly and now Pyp turns to Sam for comfort and advice. Sam knows the odds are stacked against them, but he offers a sort of fatherly arm to reassure him. The instinctive feeling Sam has to take over rather than be deterred by his own lack of confidence is when he really shines.

[ABOVE] *Ygritte dies in the arms of her crow.* [FOLLOWING SPREAD] *The wildlings are engulfed in flames during the attack on the Wall.*

CHILDREN OF THE FOREST:
A BRIEF HISTORY

"THE FIRST MEN CALLED US THE CHILDREN. WE WERE BORN LONG BEFORE THEM."

—CHILD OF THE FOREST

LITTLE IS KNOWN OF THE "DAWN AGE," the time when Westeros was home to the Children of the Forest. For untold thousands of years they lived amongst the trees and worshipped the Old Gods, in the godswood, carving faces into the weirwood trees and living in harmony with nature.

Then, over twelve thousand years ago, the First Men crossed a land bridge from Essos and spread across Westeros. As the First Men cut down the trees for their settlements, they sparked a war with the Children of the Forest. For centuries, the invaders' bronze swords clashed with the Children's obsidian blades until a truce was brokered, and the two people signed an accord known as the Pact on the Isle of Faces. Peace reigned, ushering in the Age of Heroes, during which the First Men adopted the Old Gods as their own. Then, about eight thousand years ago, when the Long Night

descended and the White Walkers invaded Westeros, the Children of the Forest and the First Men fought together to drive the undead wights back into the uncharted Lands of Always Winter.

A period of peace followed until the invasion of the Andals, who arrived about six thousand years ago. The Andals drove the First Men from every part of Westeros and brought with them the religion of the Seven, conquering all but the North and massacring the Children, who were seen as abominations. Believed to have been exterminated, all that seemed to remain of the Children was the faith of the Old Gods and stories of magic retained by the North and its people.

[ABOVE] *The Child guides Bran and his party into the cave.* [OPPOSITE] *Bran's visions and his powers become prolific.*

BRAN'S VISIONS

"HE'S WAITING FOR YOU. WE HAVE TO FIND IT. YOU NEED TO MAKE IT."

—JOJEN REED TO BRAN STARK

Ever since Jojen Reed first appeared with his sister, Meera, he has been helping guide Bran (Isaac Hempstead-Wright) to follow his visions. The trio escape north of the Wall, but the small group's battles are far from over—Jojen is weakening, and they have no clear destination. Bran is torn between the freedom he experiences when he wargs and inhabits his direwolf and the stark warnings from Jojen that Bran is losing his humanity by doing so. Then, in one moment, everything changes. While stopping to rest in a forest, Bran touches a weirwood and his visions descend—the past and present collide, along with a glimpse of the future. Bran is left with one final, frightening image: he now knows both the location they must travel to in order to meet his destiny as well as the sacrifice it will take to get there. The image he sees is of two distinctive, massive weirwood trees growing amongst four clear peaks.

When they finally reach their destination, it seems like the group might find refuge until, at the last moment, wights attack with a violence not seen before. To escape to safety, Bran must warg into Hodor's mind once more to aid Meera in the fight, but Jojen cannot be saved and to prevent him from turning, Meera has no choice but to grant her beloved brother the only mercy left, a swift and clean death.

ISAAC HEMPSTEAD-WRIGHT (BRAN STARK): I think the sad thing for Bran is that he would have known that this had to happen. As devastating and tragic as Jojen's death is, it's not something unexpected in this world, where so much requires sacrifice. He's had to move on from his brother Rickon and leave Jon behind at Craster's to reach this place. He knows he has to get to the place he has foreseen.

ALEX GRAVES (DIRECTOR): It was important to me that this scene be truly awful. The added element of having Meera kill her own brother to save the group, to have them running through the caves with this shadow over them, was great drama.

DAVID BENIOFF AND D. B. WEISS (CO-EXECUTIVE PRODUCERS AND WRITERS): We don't want to get into too much detail about why these are different, because . . . well, those are questions that the show itself will answer down the road. But yes, when he lost his legs, he gained something else. And that something else makes him a very important person.

— BUILDING THE CAVE OF ROOTS —

After a monumental struggle through the unforgiving landscape of the North, Bran Stark and his companions finally reach the home of his visions and the location of a mysterious power, found within the Cave of Roots. As they approach, the group is beset by wights, *older and more grotesque than ever before, and the skirmish costs Jojen Reed his life. Afterward, the group is ushered into the cave by a Child of the Forest and guided to Bran's destiny—to meet the Three-Eyed Raven.*

DEB RILEY (PRODUCTION DESIGNER): David and Dan really know what they want. It's all about finding the right tone. We started by introducing a light source within the cave, but ultimately it looked too sci-fi, so we had to take it out. We have to keep the base of reality, the gritty, dirty feel of the cave—even though it is inhabited by a man woven into the roots.

TOM MARTIN (CONSTRUCTION MANAGER): This was a very interesting build that started on location in a quarry north of Belfast. We excavated hundreds of tons of earth to build the approach and the entrance to the cave. Then in the studio we built the tunnels leading to the main part of the cave. The tunnels themselves were over eighty feet long and built on different levels with a very wet and organic feel to the walls and floor. Our fantastic greens department spent weeks stripping and wire brushing thousands of individual roots before securing them to the walls and heavy-duty rigs hung from the stage roof. Once all of this was in place, the roots had to be individually painted to give a natural organic feeling to the set, but also to allow light to reflect off the roots, giving everything a fantastical look. The floor was then covered in a mixture of clay and compost and dressed with dozens of skulls and hundreds of bones.

MIKE GIBSON (GREENS DEPARTMENT): There was a bit of a struggle to find the right material—we could have created foam roots, but the cost would have been prohibitive especially given the size of the set. We discovered that rhododendron branches were perfect for creating the gnarled and twisted feel we were looking for. Rhododendron can be quite invasive to woodlands and has to be cleared. The site for another set gave us permission to take away some of their cleared branches. The next challenge was how these branches would be fixed onto the set as it was built. Basically, we suspended everything from the massive scaffolding that construction had built around the set. For three weeks, we had three guys and a truck driver collecting and delivering branches constantly from three different forests. Each of the roots was individually sanded, placed, and painted. The screws alone cost around a thousand pounds. On top of all that, the cave was then finished with twenty tons of soil and ten tons of rock.

ISAAC HEMPSTEAD-WRIGHT (BRAN STARK): That set is spectacular. Crawling through the bones was the coolest thing ever. I felt like I was on a heavy-metal music video set. It was one of my favorite moments of the season.

[ABOVE] *To reach the end of the journey, Bran must continue alone.*
[OPPOSITE] *Bran and his party enter the Cave of Roots.*

— CREATING THE THREE-EYED RAVEN —

"I'VE BEEN MANY THINGS. NOW I AM WHAT YOU SEE."

—THE THREE-EYED RAVEN

For as long as Bran Stark has had visions, he has been visited by the power behind the visions of the Three-Eyed Raven, which seems to guide him ever closer to a fate untold. Bran hoped that upon meeting the Raven, he might have the power to restore his ability to walk, but it is not to be. The only promise he makes to Bran is that one day he will fly.

BARRIE GOWER (PROSTHETICS SUPERVISOR): From the beginning, this character really got my juices flowing. I knew it was going to need the most collaboration between the departments because we were building this character into a set. The character is effectively suspended in a lattice of roots, so we needed to be able to keep the actor safe, but also make it possible for him to get in and out fairly easily between takes.

Early on, I was thinking about the work that Tom Savini did on all these classic 1980s horror movies, like *Friday the 13th* and *Dawn of the Dead*. Someone would be decapitated, or lying on a slab with their organs coming out, and the way that was achieved was to have a false body with a board positioned either under or behind. All the actor needed to do was put his head through a well-positioned gap. That's what we ended up doing—the actor used his head,

shoulders, and arms, but the rest of the body was fabricated and incorporated into the set. Our actor then climbed a ladder and slid into position. All we had to do was dress final branches around his body.

The set itself was one of the most gob-smacking sets I have ever been on. To be there, incorporating our work into it, was a huge moment for us. It can be a challenge to have to match something that is real, but on the day of the shoot, people were stepping around all the roots unsure of what was real or fake—it felt like a real success. The set was lit perfectly, and when they started to pump in the dry ice, it was like being in another world.

[OPPOSITE] *The Three-Eyed Raven woven in the roots.*

[ABOVE] *The weirwood tree—the end point of the journey of Bran's visions.*

— EPILOGUE: ADDING TO ARYA'S PRAYER —

"Joffrey. Cersei. Walder Frey. Meryn Trant. Tywin Lannister. The Red Woman. Beric Dondarrion. Thoros of Myr. Ilyn Payne. The Mountain. The Hound."

—Arya Stark

Arya's nightly ritual includes reciting a list of names of people that she plans to find and kill. During my interviews, I asked each person, not who they thought would successfully secure the crown (or, let's be honest, survive) in Game of Thrones, but who, for themselves or their character, should be added to the list and become marked for death.

MAISIE WILLIAMS (ARYA STARK): Melisandre. Some of the other characters are almost admirable, even in their evil twisted ways—but I can see nothing redeeming in her character! Whatever she says her motivations are—I'm not buying it.

ROSE LESLIE (YGRITTE): It's got to be Littlefinger. He's the one who scares me the most. He's more terrifying than Joffrey, who is just an evil little kid. He's so clever and manipulative, and truly terrible.

CHARLES DANCE (TYWIN LANNISTER): Littlefinger. He has to go—he's so oily. He's like a gas that you can't see or touch, but it gets into your respiratory system and you don't know anything about it until it's too late. He's such a wonderfully Machiavellian character. I wouldn't want to see him survive too long.

SIBEL KEKILLI (SHAE): Walder Frey. I hate him for killing everyone at the Red Wedding. I have a list! Kill him, kill him, that one's got to go . . . I could go on. Roose Bolton is awful, and Shae wouldn't be too happy that Littlefinger has Sansa now—he's really, really dangerous. Sorry, Lena, I love you, but Cersei is the monster of it all for me.

DIANA RIGG (OLENNA TYRELL): No matter what they are doing, I'd rather keep everyone alive! I rather like the dynamics as they are.

ISAAC HEMPSTEAD-WRIGHT (BRAN STARK): I don't trust Melisandre, but I'm not sure I'd want her dead—maybe just imprisoned somewhere in a dungeon. Ramsay Snow, the torture boy, for me I think.

JACOB ANDERSON (GREY WORM): I really wanted Joffrey to die, but I think I'm going to miss how much I loved hating him, that evil little bastard. But you know who should really die? Roose Bolton.

IAN MCELHINNEY (BARRISTAN SELMY): It would be an aberration, to put it mildly, if Cersei were to make it in the end, but I expect we'll be stuck with her for a while.

PEDRO PASCAL (OBERYN MARTELL): As Oberyn, it's delightful that Tywin goes down this season. As an audience member, I was thrilled to be able to watch Joffrey die, and then I met Jack [Gleeson] and he is the antithesis of his character. I sort of love Joffrey now, the character he's portraying, the man he truly is.

LENA HEADEY (CERSEI LANNISTER): As Cersei, probably Margaery and Tyrion in equal measure. As me? Well, I was very happy when Craster was murdered, but I'm going to have to go with Stannis.

MICHAEL MCELHATTON (ROOSE BOLTON): I'm sort of at a loss now that Tywin's gone, though I'm glad for Roose. But I'm going to have to go with Joffrey for my own self.

NATHALIE EMMANUEL (MISSANDEI): Cersei needs to get her comeuppance—even after everything with Joffrey, I feel like she's owed some justice, definitely.

RICHARD DORMER (BERIC DONDARRION): Joffrey was a monster, but getting Catelyn killed? Walder Frey is just pure evil.

SOPHIE TURNER (SANSA STARK): As a character, I think that Daenerys is such a strong player in the game, she has to die for someone else to be able to come forward. As much as I love watching her, I think she's the biggest threat.

EMILIA CLARKE (DAENERYS TARGARYEN): I know I don't want Littlefinger on the throne, but Aidan Gillen is so good and his storyline is so interesting I don't want him dead.

NIKOLAJ COSTER-WALDAU (JAIME LANNISTER): I would like to see the dragons killed. They are weapons of mass destruction. We can't have that. Horrible, horrible, evil machines of death. I have a feeling they'll probably make it, though.

PETER DINKLAGE (TYRION LANNISTER): We've lost some winners in that category this season. I'm going to have to go with Hot Pie, never trusted that kid. Roose Bolton will get his somehow, but you've got to watch out for Hot Pie.

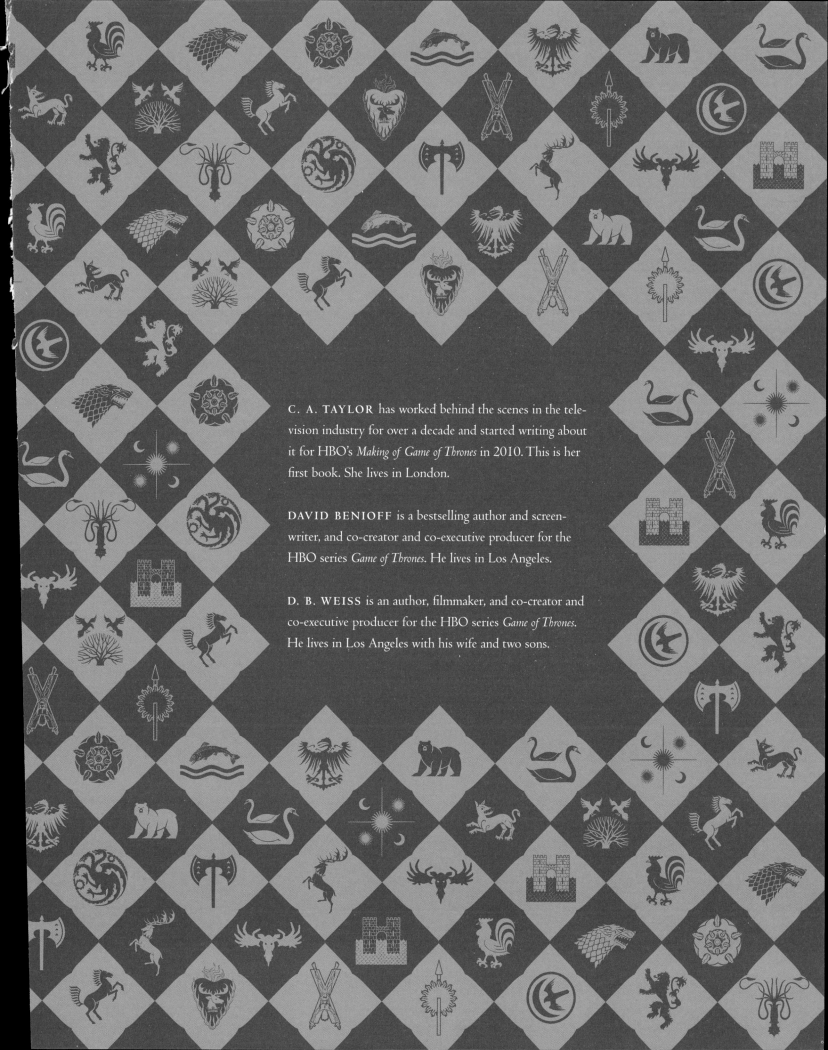

C. A. TAYLOR has worked behind the scenes in the television industry for over a decade and started writing about it for HBO's *Making of Game of Thrones* in 2010. This is her first book. She lives in London.

DAVID BENIOFF is a bestselling author and screenwriter, and co-creator and co-executive producer for the HBO series *Game of Thrones*. He lives in Los Angeles.

D. B. WEISS is an author, filmmaker, and co-creator and co-executive producer for the HBO series *Game of Thrones*. He lives in Los Angeles with his wife and two sons.